Sarah Niblock works as both a journalist and a lecturer. After graduating with an honours degree in Communication Studies, she worked as a reporter for a local newspaper. She gained her NCTJ Proficiency Certificate and joined the *Liverpool Echo* as a senior journalist before moving into lecturing. While lecturing on the University of Manchester BA (Hons) Degree in Media Studies with Business Management she developed and taught modules in Multimedia Journalism and continues to have a specific interest in advances in new technology including multimedia, CD-ROM and the Internet and the effect these developments have had on the working lives of journalists. Sarah continues to work as a freelance journalist, contributing to national broadsheet newspapers, radio and women's magazines.

Inside Journalism

CAREER BUILDERS GUIDES

Inside the Music Business
Tony Barrow and Julian Newby

Inside Book Publishing
Giles Clark

Forthcoming

Inside Broadcasting
Julian Newby

Inside Journalism

Sarah Niblock

Routledge
Taylor & Francis Group

Published by Blueprint, an imprint of Chapman & Hall

First edition 1996

Reprinted 2003
By Routledge
11 New Fetter Lane, London EC4P 4EE

Transferred to Digital Printing 2003

Routledge is an imprint of the Taylor & Francis Group

© 1996 Sarah Niblock

Typeset in 10/12 pt Palatino by Mews Photosetting, Beckenham, Kent

ISBN 1 85713 022 7

A catalogue record for this book is available from the British Library

Library of Congress Catalog Card Number: 95-79872

Printed and bound by Antony Rowe Ltd, Eastbourne

Contents

Acknowledgements

This book is dedicated to Scott Callanish.

With thanks to the following people for their input and encouragement: Simon Cadman, David Charters, Charles Chuck, Andrew Culf, Ken Dennis, Nigel Everitt, John Griffith, Niki Hinman, John Holden, Ian Jolley, David Longbottom, Maria McGeoghan, Iain Mann, Jessany Marsden, Terry Moore, Charles Morrissey, John Pullin, Janet Tansley, Paul Walker, Ivor Yorke and to the countless organizations who assisted with this book.

Foreword

It did not need Watergate, or even the fall of the Berlin Wall, to convince the world of the benefits of a free, independent journalistic tradition for a just and democratic society. For long before these events, journalists have been shaping the language, thoughts and politics of the world at large. Through characterisation in books and films, journalism has long held a hint of glamour to young cub reporter and hack alike with the thrill of the scoop, the power to shape global or local perception of events.

However, journalism in the 1990s is also big business – strategic, competitive and occasionally cut-throat – the endeavour and lifeblood of thousands each day and night. The recent upsurge of interest in the journalistic profession reflects the powerful growth of the media industry, driven by the over-hyped convergence of audio-visual, telecommunications and computing technologies to create the world of 'multimedia' and the 'information superhighway'. Media is currently at a crossroads, getting to grips with new technologies and working practices, and prey to public and regulatory concerns over cross-media ownership and the invasion of privacy.

Given these uncertainties, it is worth pausing to reflect on the solid progress and achievements that have brought journalism to its current evolved state, a state we tend to take for granted as we read our daily broadsheet or watch the late evening news. A good starting point is Sarah Niblock's authoritative and detailed profile of today's industry, its diverse techniques, its various individual roles and routes of entry to the profession. It provides an essential guide for all aspiring journalists seeking to navigate the journalistic rapids in pursuit of career rewards. It is also a fascinating account of real-life journalism for the curious reader.

The skills demanded of today's journalist are ever widening. Yes, you must have the traditional enquiring mind, individual spark and dogged determination but you also need to be conversant with the finer points of law, to understand the latest in production technology and develop man-management skills to help you co-ordinate the efforts of a wider team. The journalist as editor must also balance his or her own sense of professional integrity against the profit goals of the business, not always an easy task.

Despite all the excitement about new technologies, and the explosive growth of new forms of communication and learning such as the Internet, the essential role of the journalist is as it has always been, to dig out the facts and then relate them clearly and accurately with added comment and colour as required. It is what makes people tick that readers, listeners and viewers find endlessly fascinating.

Lord Clive Hollick
Group Managing Director
MAI plc – International Financial, Media
and Information Services

1

Introduction

It is six o'clock on a freezing February morning. The news reporter has just arrived for work and is perusing the morning papers over a coffee. The 'phone rings and it's an alert member of the public saying a train has been derailed. Many passengers have been injured and the disaster area is swarming with police, fire and ambulance crews. It's all systems go ... the start of another busy media day.

WHAT IS JOURNALISM?

Journalism, be it working for newspapers, magazines, radio or television, is a 365-day, 24-hour operation going on just about everywhere in the world. Whether you are reading this in the middle of the day or night, journalists are hard at work preparing bulletins, writing features, producing documentaries, designing pages and editing tape ready for their next deadline. Stories can be totally unpredictable and crop up when you least expect them to. You don't stop being a journalist at 5pm. It is not just a job, it's a way of life and you are always on the look-out for a new idea.

When we turn on our television sets, tune in the radio or glance at today's front pages, we see names and faces which are almost as famous as the people in their stories. Indeed, journalism is a profession surrounded by mystique and glamour. But those most visible practitioners at the very top represent only a tiny fraction of journalists. There are literally hundreds of thousands of people working in the media in an enormous range of roles. This vast realm of journalism covers not only news but also documentaries, features, photojournalism, business and commerce and entertainment information.

The interesting thing is that while the media is now part of our everyday lives, we rarely see what goes on to produce articles and programmes or know who the key players are. This book is an attempt to describe the nature of the wide range of jobs in the media and to enable potential journalists to steer their way around the myriad of paths leading to a career.

Media unlimited

While the scope of topics covered by journalists is unlimited, it is also the case that the range of media available to convey these stories is also expanding. This book will concentrate on the traditional media forms – newspapers, magazines, radio and television – with the addition of agencies, freelancing and public relations. But you will also read how the boundaries between all these media are blurring with the far-reaching developments in computer technology. More on that later.

Millions of newspapers are ready every day and they remain not only one of our primary sources of news and current affairs but are also a form of entertainment. Newspapers bring us detailed pen portraits of scenes and events taking place at home and abroad and, in their feature pages, give explanations and raise issues on topics of concern to the majority of readers. We also turn to newspapers for everyday information, from holiday sunspots to horoscopes, recipes to racing.

While newspapers have broad appeal, magazines come in many guises with mass readership or a clearly defined small market. Whoever you are or whatever you do, there is probably a periodical that will appeal to you as a reader. There are leisure and entertainment-oriented magazines, cinema and music publications and a periodical catering for just about every conceivable hobby. This book will also examine a massive sector of the magazine market, business and professional periodicals which serve the interests of those working in industry and commerce.

No household is without at least one radio because it can be listened to while you do other things. One of the strengths of radio as a journalistic medium is its portability which means radio is often the first source of information for people listening in their cars, on their personal stereos or just around the house. The popularity of radio is demonstrated by the rise of new stations catering not just for mass audiences but for specialist interests also.

With its ability to harness words, sound and pictures, television has immense impact for journalism. By appealing to many of our senses, major issues are beamed straight into our living rooms and seem more real and immediate than reading about them or listening to them.

As you will read, there are thousands of journalists working in each of these media. But there is also a growing number of journalists who choose to work one step removed from the mainstream organizations and instead provide a service to the media. These are people who work in news agencies and who operate independently as freelances who supply stories for publication and broadcast. In addition, there are those who not only want to report the news, they want to make the news. These people work in public relations, bringing to the media's attention issues and events for coverage.

But before any hopeful candidate starts enrolling for courses or applying for jobs in any of these media, they have to equip themselves with skills fundamental to all journalists whatever medium they are working in. That includes good judgment as to what issues or events make good stories, how to gather the facts and details essential to the topic being covered and how to structure stories in a way that makes them interesting, factual and unbiased. All these issues will be dealt with in this introduction along with a glimpse at some of the other characteristics and skills you can develop to help you on your career path. It is advisable, therefore, to read this chapter before embarking on other sections as it will help you to understand the mechanics of specific media. In this chapter and throughout the rest of the book, you will find useful and unique advice from journalists working at the very top of their respective media, plus case studies to illustrate how stories are put together.

First, let us examine that most fundamental of journalistic questions ...

What makes a good story?

Dictionary definition of news: report of recent happenings, tidings; interesting facts not previously known.

Ask any journalist how they would define 'news' and most would find it a very hard question to answer. The term 'newsworthiness' is used by journalists to describe any event or issue meriting coverage whether it be as a front-page headline on a daily newspaper or a half-hour radio documentary. Skilled journalists are often too intimately involved with their craft to be able to stand back dispassionately and analyse what they do. It is often a personal process and deciding what to cover relies on gut, human reaction. Journalists, academics, readers, viewers and listeners invariably clash over the invisible criteria used to determine why some events become stories while others go unreported. Journalists maintain they are responding to what the public wants, while theorists argue that news is managed and constructed to suit the needs of people in powerful positions, from politicians to advertisers. Regardless, anyone working in a newsroom or hoping to make a career out of journalism must have a clear understanding of newsworthiness even if, as is often the case with the most senior, experienced news people, they cannot articulate what news is.

Lord Reith, first General Manager and later Director General of the BBC, developed the principle that it was the duty of the new medium of broadcasting 'to inform, to educate and to entertain'. This is still the main objective of journalists today although to what degree they concentrate on one or more of these is debatable. No matter whether they are cookery writers for a women's magazine, war correspondents for a national news agency or bulletin editors on a local radio station, journalists are aiming to grab the readers' attention, stimulate and inform them. Most members of society have a natural interest and a healthy curiosity in those changes that affect their personal lives. At a national level, we will be affected by a new rate of income tax, a spell of severe weather or a strike by train drivers. There are other factors which people look to the media for as well as information – entertainment and leisure. So journalism may not only touch our physical lives but may also inspire, amuse or outrage us. It is a highly responsible and demanding task.

Perhaps the best place to start unravelling the definition of news stories is to consider the words themselves. **New(s)**, those first three letters mean so much as it is often the closeness, or newness, of the event to the time of publication or broadcast that determines whether it will be mediated. Then there is **story**. All journalists are acting as story tellers, relating to the rest of us what has taken place and, possibly, why. It is that very selection, packaging and delivery that transforms something from being a happening to becoming a story.

Most journalists maintain there is no mystique in selecting a story topic from the countless mundane events that make up our everyday lives. A news producer for television network Sky News says:

> You don't think about it too deeply or intellectually, you just know as it's a very personal thing. You first decide an event's interest value. It's a very basic measure but if something makes me think 'oh really' or 'blimey, did you see that' or 'how dare he' or 'isn't that awful', it is news. It's that kind of human emotion that you use and anybody you'll meet in a cafe or pub will tell you what is interesting, so it is not something special to the job of being a journalist.

Journalists might cover something very good – human achievement, medical breakthroughs, the latest box-office hit – or something very bad like murders, tragic accidents or factory closures. There are important reasons for this if you try to disentangle the tight web of factors that determine what is reported. These are some of the questions a journalist may ask of a story:

1. **Does it involve human beings?** You may have heard of the term human interest angle which is simply the way a journalist will introduce the event to their audience to evoke a response. If a new factory is opening, the story will lead on how many job opportunities are created rather than how efficient the machinery is, simply because the human implications are ones that we can sympathize or empathize with. Any story which is likely to evoke emotion, whether it is happiness or sadness, anger or delight, on the part of the reader is more likely to be included. Events involving injury or death are newsworthy because of the value we place on the sanctity of human life. That goes for vulnerable members of society, too, which is why we are more likely to see a story reported about a child or an elderly person than someone who is middle-aged.

2. **What is the scale of the event?** The more people are involved or implicated in an occurrence, the more chance it will attract an audience. That is why anything to do with the Government is reported because laws affect all of us. Disasters with major

human costs will also hit the headlines because of the numbers involved. Scale might also apply to money, particularly if some-one has won – or stolen – a massive amount.

3. Is it unexpected? It goes without saying that if an event happens out-of-the-blue it is more likely to take us by surprise and get a reaction than if we had been expecting it. Unfortunately, a lot of what we might term bad news happens unpredictably, which is why so much of it is in the headlines. A proportion of major news, however, is predicted and can be pre-pared ahead with reporters knowing precisely where they will be going and what is expected of them, for instance a major trial, a council meeting or a news conference held by a big multination-al organization.

4. Is it relevant to the audience? For a story to be newsworthy, it needs to mean something to its audience which can vary depending upon the medium. Relevance in journalism can rely on factors such as geography, gender, occupation, age and inter-ests. The sheer range of journalistic material available should give you some idea of the diversity of the market. A local weekly newspaper in Scunthorpe is unlikely to report upon a super-market robbery in Birmingham, unless, that is, the manager is a local person which would make the story of human interest to its readers. A business-to-business periodical aimed at engineers is unlikely to run as its front-page lead story a new medical break-through. On a very basic level, a national tabloid newspaper will opt for a more sensational story than a broadsheet simply because its proprietor and journalists know that that is what will attract its particular readership.

You will read in this book how every medium has a different agenda for different reasons. Television is largely led by pictures and therefore stations may raise the status of a story if there is some sensational footage to go with it. Radio, by virtue of its reliance on sound, is more flexible. Editors find it easier to break into programmes with news flashes and a lead story does not necessarily have to be anything more than a single voice telling listeners what has happened. Like television though less so, newspapers and magazines are visual so pictures can determine a story's placing. The time involved in the printing process, although short when compared with methods used only a few years ago, means that newspapers and periodicals will aim to tell the story behind the news or issue rather than always be first to break it, with the exception of a special exclusive story or investigation.

Similarly, if you are working for an international news agency, supplying the first reports to all media on a coup in a remote part of the globe, you view the world completely differently to the way you view it from, say, a local radio station for which a comparatively minor event occurring on their doorstep is likely to take priority. Newsworthiness and the work of a journalist therefore depends on what paper, magazine, programme or station he or she works for as much as the potential story itself. Journalists cannot assess the newsworthiness of a story in a vacuum; they must always consider who they are telling it to and how interested that audience will be. To illustrate this, here is an account by one journalist on how he determines what is covered. His account gives some insight as to how personal a decision it is.

Head of News, national network radio news agency

'The first rule of journalism is to know your audience otherwise you won't be in tune with them. Local radio stations and local newspaper offices tend to be closer to their audiences. Most journalists have very fond memories of their readers walking through the door of their office and telling them face-to-face what they thought of a story. At local level, you are very close to your audience but by the time you get to national level it is easy to forget exactly for whom you are writing. On the other hand, readers probably look at national papers with different expectations than those they have of their local papers.

'I would suggest that to be a good journalist, you have to have an innately inquisitive nature, a sense of wanting to know what's going on around you and caring about it. A lot of people have this sense but then you need to be able to develop this skill and learn how to adapt it. News is creating interesting stories about things going on in our lives and presenting those stories so that large numbers of people will

> be interested. You can have good news which is interesting.
> But the fact is that, by nature, human beings tend to see
> baddies as the anti-heroes and therefore as interesting people.
> If news was about the usual you'd be bored rigid. After years
> of experience it becomes second nature to a journalist to
> know what makes news, and I would recommend journalists
> not to analyse what they do because you are in danger of
> fudging what you are trying to do. I hate the word but you
> do need to decide on your 'priorities', and this is an ability peo-
> ple improve as they come into a national newsroom like this.
> You start off by thinking, would this story interest someone in
> Manchester as well as in Inverness? With experience, that
> thought process happens in about one-and-a-half seconds.'

Understanding what makes news is to some extent innate in all
of us. As social beings we unknowingly categorize life into the
usual and unusual and use our emotions to help us make sense
of the world to ourselves and other people. But what makes
people journalists is something extra. They need to know how to
mediate that information to other people. This is something that
involves a mixture of skills, training and experience, some of
which will be described in this book.

The pleasures of working in journalism are not just about the
people you interview or the stories you cover in the course of
your day. Working in a busy editorial department is one of the
most exciting and satisfying experiences you can have; for the
interaction with colleagues as you work in an intense environment as much as the spontaneity of the issues you encounter.

The changing working environment

The working environment for a journalist is barely recognizable
when compared with newspaper, magazine and broadcast offices
as recently as 10 or 20 years ago. Films depicting shabby rooms,
with raincoat-clad hacks hunched over old typewriters surrounded by overflowing wastebins is not too distanced from the
reality of media establishments a decade or so ago. Now, in most
cases the clattering of typewriters has been replaced by the much
quieter clicking of computer keyboards, with barely a sheet of
paper to be seen. But while the surroundings are much more

modern (and many lament the loss of the atmospheric old news-rooms) the fundamentals of the job have changed very little over the decades.

From the end of the First World War until the technological revolution of the 1970s and '80s, there was remarkable uni-formity and continuity in journalism. A journalist beginning their career even as late as the early 1980s was schooled by older pro-fessionals who may have begun their working lives in the 1920s and '30s. And the skills they taught these junior reporters – such as note-taking and cultivating loyal contacts – are as relevant and fundamental to the work of journalists today as they ever were.

It is higher up the production ladder where changes in work-ing routines are most evident and this is mainly the result of new technology. In newspapers, whole departments have been wiped out as computers transform print production methods. In broad-casting, the razor-blade and chalk style of editing has been replaced by sophisticated digital machines.

The journalist's job

Many would-be journalists are attracted to the media because they enjoy writing. Sadly the literary-minded are often disappointed when they discover they have around five minutes to compose a hefty story and are restricted to the simplest English. That is because unless you have the privilege of being a columnist or working in some other area of journalism that permits lengthy prose, most of the reporter's time is spent on the telephone or out in the field. But for the majority who choose to make a career out of journalism, that is the most exciting part. It sounds a cliché but being there when history is unfolding is a remarkable experience.

The job of a journalist is a three-phase thing and not simply down to sitting at a keyboard all day and writing as so many mis-takenly believe. It requires:

1. **Researching:** news is about knowing what information is required for the story and where to lay your hands on those facts quickly. You have to be informed about current affairs and know who are the key players in a variety of areas so that you can judge instantly the swiftest and most profitable research route.
2. **Judgment:** unless you can judge how to treat the material, you may be a good researcher or writer, but not a good journalist.

Judgment involves knowing how important the story is to readers. What sort of information should be included? How should the story be structured – as a two-paragraph filler or a half-page feature, a headline or an 'and finally ... '? Should it be accompanied by pictures or audio? Good judgment means being able, perhaps with only the first, limited information about a story, to visualize it in the context of a finished page or bulletin.

3. **Presentation:** following on from the last point, once you have the information you have to know how best to mediate it to your audience, a skill which will be determined by who you are working for as much as by your own command of the English language.

The practical application of these stages in every medium is the development of contacts, interviewing skills, application of the law and the ability to write.

Contact/sources

Where information comes from is the aspect that dominates most journalists' working lives. If a journalist cannot get a story or the necessary information in to back it up, they cannot mediate the facts to the public. A contacts book is the journalist's most guarded and private possession because it contains the names, addresses and telephone numbers of everyone who can provide details or comment upon any issue or event they cover. Stories are gathered from information gleaned by journalists from members of the public, commercial companies, agencies such as local authorities, emergency services, charities, schools, hospitals, Government departments, industry, commerce, pressure groups, professional organizations, political parties, the list is endless. Contacts books come in various guises and rapidly grow in size as the journalist builds their career and encounters more helpful people. Some choose a small ring-bound folder so that they can insert extra pages as they make more contacts. Many journalists carry portable computers and will store their contacts' names and numbers on their VDU.

A great deal of time is spent by journalists finding stories by contacting organizations and individuals directly. The relationship between journalists and their contacts is double-edged: the journalist needs the story and the contact is likely to want publicity.

Interviewing skills

All journalists have to know how to conduct successful interviews in person or on the telephone. Personal interviews conducted either face-to-face or over the telephone are the main way in which journalists get their information. Even when the story is obtained another way, such as from a letter, the journalist must still speak to individuals involved to check the facts and 'flesh out' details to make interesting copy. The art of interviewing is an essential skill for all journalists and it can be learned even by the shy or tongue-tied. Often, you have no choice but to interview someone at very short notice. With experience, this becomes second nature but for the beginner it is better to prepare for the interview in advance.

In an interview it is important for the journalist to direct the conversation so they gather the details they require quickly and fully and are not driven off the point by a forceful interviewee who may be trying to duck the issue. This is achieved through preparation. Likewise, by being prepared, you will appear more confident which may put a nervous interviewee at ease. The first thing a journalist must do after making the appointment is to find out as many background details about the subject as they can. Most media organizations keep a back catalogue of newspaper cuttings which are filed under subject titles for this purpose. The next step is to jot down a few essential questions to use as reference so you do not miss anything vital to the story. These questions are meant to be a guide as the path of the interview might change or the interviewee may answer them before they are asked. The main questions that need to be answered in all stories are **who, what, when, where, why** and **how**? These have to be tailored to suit the story. For example, who is raising the petition? Where exactly will the supermarket be built? When are you planning to release your next album? What exactly did you see? How did the child come to be playing in that road? Why didn't doctors spot this earlier? Most questions should be open-ended, which means they cannot be answered with a straight yes or no. The best stories contain sections where the interviewee is allowed to describe the situation in their own words.

When it comes to carrying out the interview itself, journalists must always be sure they are speaking to the right person as there might be two John Smiths living in the same road. They must also identify themselves clearly so the interviewee knows they are talking to a journalist and that their words will be reported. As long as your contact is clear they are talking to a journalist for publication or broadcast, whatever they say can be used and attributed to them. If however, they tell the journalist that what they are about to say is 'off the record', they mean that they do not want it written down or broadcast. For example, the interviewee might have some background information about a subject which, if divulged publicly, might jeopardize their job.

The basis of a good interview is a friendly, positive manner on the part of the journalist. The golden rule is to remember you may have to speak to them again next week. The journalist must always be polite and calm and tailor their approach according to the circumstances. It is best to keep as much eye contact with the interviewee as possible. This is considered polite practice with the added factor that you might also catch facial expressions that would lead you to believe the interviewee is not telling you the whole truth. This is much easier for broadcast journalists who will use a microphone or camera to record the information. Print journalists are usually trained in Teeline shorthand which enables them to jot down details quickly, or they use a mini-cassette recorder.

All journalists will inevitably encounter problem interviews. A typical case is where a hassled official replies 'I don't know' or 'no comment' to a probing question. Here, the reporter has to employ assertiveness skills to try to draw out the information. This may involve politely repeating a question or re-expressing it in a way that might elicit a response.

At the end of the interview, the journalist might wish to go over the facts of the story with the interviewee again to check they have understood them correctly. They should also ensure they have several paragraphs or extracts of directly quoted speech before they begin to write their story. As a reminder:

1. make an appointment;
2. prepare by researching interviewee/subject;
3. write out a list of questions;
4. identify yourself and ensure you are interviewing the right person;
5. be friendly, positive and polite;
6. check facts.

Writing ability

There is an art to writing copy that will attract an audience and keep them interested while remaining unbiased. Journalism involves one of the most disciplined forms of writing and is a skill that is mastered by reading or listening to others' work as often as possible and through dedicated practice. While they are known as stories, articles are not written in the same way as the stories you might read in a book. Whereas you might have to wait with baited breath until the very last page of a novel for the plot's climax, the most important information in an article should be contained in the first few paragraphs. That is why journalism is frequently described as a conversational form of writing: if you were verbally describing to a friend an incident you had seen on the way to the supermarket, you would be likely to mention the most attention-grabbing aspect first. It works exactly the same way with journalism because your aim is to grab the audience's attention.

Before they start writing, journalists must consider three golden rules which are:

- accuracy,

- conciseness,

- clarity.

Accuracy is essential. If a journalist reports inaccurate information, they and their newspaper or station may be sued for libel or prosecuted under Contempt of Court laws. Even if a name is misspelled, it ruins the journalist's integrity with their contact as it appears that they are careless.

News, in particular, should always be written concisely because pressure of space and airtime means journalists must convey the maximum amount of information in the fewest words. This is also better for the audience as they are able to glean the information easily and quickly without having to plough through irrelevant detail. Paragraphs in journalistic writing are only a couple of sentences long and the language within them is simple and clear so that concepts will be mediated in as few words with as little punctuation as possible. For example, instead of writing 'Freda Smith, who works as the Director of Education in the city Bigtown, replied by commenting ...' a journalist would put 'Bigtown Education Director Freda Smith said ...'.

If language must be clear and concise in journalistic writing, it follows that the content of the story itself must be easily understood. The reader should not be in any doubt about the facts of the story; there should be no ambiguities. This clarity is achieved by structuring stories in a particular way so the reader is certain from the beginning what the main point of the issue or event is:

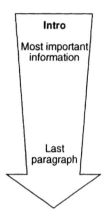

The story should consist of relevant facts, the answers to the questions **who, what, where, when, why** and **how**, interspersed with directly quoted material, which is marked off as in quotation marks. These are the interviewees' owns words or recorded speech for broadcast. Quotes, as they are called, add credibility and authenticity to the piece as well as providing relief and interest. The most important paragraph in a story is the introduction because this must convey the main point of the piece, the angle. This is the narrative standpoint taken by the journalist on the strength of the news values upon which the story is based. Writers use their judgment to consider what aspect of the event or issue will be of most interest to their audience. Having written the introduction, the journalist unfolds the rest of the story, leaving the least important information until the last couple of paragraphs. This is a common practice in newspaper journalism where a ruthless sub-editor, who has the task of fitting the story into a page layout, may simply cut off the last few sentences if short of space and time.

News journalists are required to endeavour to report objectively, which means they must not express an opinion or any bias in favour of any of the conflicting sides of a story. Their role is to convey facts and represent all sides in an argument fairly, and, ultimately, to allow the reader or listener to make an informed judgment on the basis of the facts presented. This is not an easy aim to achieve when you consider the range of stories a journalist might cover. Some issues are so emotive it is almost impossible not to convey your own anger or disbelief.

Other types of journalists, such as those who write features or columns, are allowed to express their opinions because it is clear that their pieces are separate from the objective, factual news content of the day. It is important to stress that while newspapers and magazines have scope for expressing opinions, there are strict laws which prevent radio and television from bias in their news output.

In writing their piece, the journalist will always be conscious of the laws affecting their work. As a reminder:

1. be accurate, concise and clear;
2. keep sentences and paragraphs short;
3. the introduction is the most important paragraph;
4. stay objective.

So now that you have an insight into the fundamental questions asked by prospective journalists and the skills and attributes common to all those working in the profession regardless of the medium, we can start to examine newspapers, magazines, radio, television and other forms of journalism in more detail. To help you, there are four main topics covered by the rest of this book which are as follows:

1. an introduction to the structure of media institutions in newspapers, magazines, radio and television;
2. the practices of journalists employed by them;
3. a glimpse into the future to examine how developments in new technology may affect the working lives of journalists;
4. suggestions as to training opportunities and routes into employment in journalism, plus advice on writing CVs, application letters and gaining work experience.

Each chapter is dedicated to a specific medium and examines how the area is owned and controlled, how stories are generated and produced with detailed examples, descriptions of the jobs of key personnel within that sector followed by training routes relevant to that medium.

Chapters on specific media are self-contained so that, if you have a particular interest in magazines, you will obtain relevant information about ownership, working practices, job descriptions and training in that area just from that section. But it is worth bearing in mind that while this book may be organized as such, no medium is separate from another. Newspapers will influence and inform radio and vice versa, for instance. Computer buffs say that in the near future we'll be taking bytes of information from the Internet, hitching a ride on the information superhighway, maybe stopping for a while at the cybercafe. Maybe we will, or maybe we'll still be calling into the newsagent for our daily paper and turning on the TV or radio. However bizarre or familiar our news and current affairs consumption may be in the future, and speculation is rife, there is no escaping the inevitable effect new technology is having and will have on the working lives of journalists. The ethos bound up in journalism – of facts, objectivity and human interest – is likely to remain for the most part. The basic tasks of reporters are going to stay, certainly for the time being. But what will change is other skills and practical attributes necessary for doing the job. So how can the aspiring journalist prepare for the future and what are the demands likely to be? The sections at the end of each chapter will deal on a basic level with some of the changes anticipated by employers and working journalists across the media which may give some insight. As we prepare to set foot on the information superhighway, there is no doubt that physical demarcations that may currently separate, say, magazines from television, might cease to be as journalists start to work in a multimedia environment where words, still and moving images and sound are united at the press of a keyboard button.

The media world resembles Spaghetti Junction. It is a big network with many crossovers and the roads all seem to lead somewhere new. To the aspiring journalist seeing the junction from overhead, it's a daunting prospect wondering which route to take into the profession. But where the roads all meet at the core of the system, common factors exist which are excellent foundations for building your career. Then you can enjoy a journey with many surprises and diversions in store.

2

Newspapers

Around 200 million newspapers are sold in the UK each week and millions more free papers are read. Britain has 21 national newspapers, 89 regional dailies and more than 1500 local weeklies. In fact nowhere in the world are newspapers read so much – for example, the British buy three times as many papers per head as France.

THE SHAPE OF THE NEWSPAPER INDUSTRY

Newspapers published in Britain fall into one of the following categories:

- **national newspapers** are sold across the whole country and give space to stories which affect or are relevant to the nation as a whole and stories from abroad;

- **regional newspapers** cover issues and events affecting one part of the country or a city, as well as giving space to the major national and international stories of the day; with one or two exceptions, such as papers distributed free to London Underground commuters, they are paid for;

- **local newspapers** report on a smaller area or community in a great deal more detail than a regional or national newspaper. An increasing number of local newspapers are funded through advertising and are distributed free to all homes and businesses within the catchment area. Others are paid for.

Very important or unusual stories, such as a murder, would be likely to be covered in all three types of paper but a scout jamboree would only be featured in the local newspaper, although it might be printed in the regional title if there was space available after the big issues had been covered.

Some national and regional titles are published daily, either early in the morning or later in the afternoon while others may only come out weekly or twice-weekly such as national Sunday newspapers and local titles. On a daily title, three or four up-dated versions, called editions, of the newspaper may be published.

National newspapers

Reading newspapers on a daily basis has been a tradition for many in the UK. Approximately 62% of us read a national each day and even more on a Sunday (figures supplied by the Newspaper Society).

Mention print and most people's minds will automatically spring to the nationals with their high-profile journalists and dynamic coverage of historic events. They employ a large staff of journalists who work from the newspaper's main office and others who are stationed in the regions and overseas.

While the staff complement may be high when compared with regional newspapers, the nationals only employ a fraction of the journalists working in Britain today so competition for jobs is fierce. It is rare, but not unknown, to find a national news-paper journalist who has not started out on a local or regional title. National reporters are almost always fully trained, experienced journalists but some titles are starting to offer graduate traineeships which teach candidates how to be reporters from scratch. Jobs on national titles are hardly ever advertised. They don't need to be because hundreds of people approach them for work every month and they can easily handpick the best candidates.

One of the main routes in is via offering stories on a freelance basis. Journalists working for regional titles who can regularly offer a national strong exclusive articles may be invited to join the staff. It takes persistence and a great deal of determination to prove you have what it takes to chase the biggest stories of the day.

With one or two exceptions, such as the *Sunday Post*, national newspapers have their main offices in London with regional offices in big cities including Manchester and Glasgow. Whereas press activity was once centred in and around Fleet Street, increasingly national titles are relocating to new purpose-built premises which may house several titles under one roof. As hot metal presses are replaced by fast, cheaper printing processes, newspapers no longer need cavernous offices. Instead, journalists are working from air-conditioned newsrooms outside the City of London with printing carried out at another site.

There are few controls over the concentration of press ownership. Almost anyone can set up a newspaper; however, ownership of papers in the UK is especially concentrated. More than 90% of national and Sunday titles rest with just five companies. The largest newspaper owner is Rupert Murdoch who controls News International, stable of the *Sun, Today, News of the World, The Times, Sunday Times* plus a host of other broadcasting and business concerns all over the world. The newspaper division of News International employs around 3600 people in the UK, the majority at its base at Wapping. The late Robert Maxwell's Mirror Group Newspapers, part of a larger international publishing concern, controls the *Daily Mirror, Daily Record* (the Mirror's Scottish sibling), the *People* and the *Sunday Mirror*. Lord Rothermere's Daily Mail and General Trust publishes the *Daily Mail, Mail on Sunday* and the *London Evening Standard*, Britain biggest regional daily. United Newspapers is responsible for the *Daily Express, Daily Star* and *Sunday Express*. Canadian Conrad Black's the Hollinger Group is majority shareholder in the *Daily Telegraph* and *Sunday Telegraph*.

Of the remaining papers, the *Sunday Sport* is independently owned, the *Financial Times* is owned by Pearson plc. The Guardian Media Group, with its national daily and regional titles, also recently took over the *Observer*. The *Independent* has been taken over by an international consortium in which Mirror Group Newspapers has a major stake.

The 21 national daily and Sunday newspapers referred to above account for the majority of those sold yet by far the highest percentage of news journalism, in the region of more than 80%, is practised outside London. News does not just happen in the capital as thousands of reporters who work round the clock in the regions will testify. In fact, it is fair to say that regional and local newspapers are frequently a source of inspiration for the nationals and certainly serve as the main training ground for would-be daily reporters.

Regional and local newspapers

Regional newspapers cover a large geographical area such as a large town or city and its surrounding villages. These papers will usually be published daily, either in the morning, as in the case of the Cardiff-based *Western Mail,* or in the late afternoon or evening, such as the *Coventry Evening Telegraph.* The regional press provides both the big national and international stories of the day coupled with local news, features and other details, such as advertising, of specific interest to its own readership.

Local newspapers cover a smaller geographical area in most cases and will be published once or twice a week. Some are paid for but the majority are delivered free-of-charge throughout the catchment area to guarantee circulation so they can attract sufficient advertising revenue. Advertising–editorial ratios in local free distribution titles, or freesheets as they are often called, are high and frequently in excess of 60:40.

The regional and local press is lively and diverse and has a responsibility to reflect and articulate the concerns of its readers in a way that national newspapers cannot. It plays a major campaigning role and can spearhead significant charitable and community initiatives. Because of its place within a community, the regional press tends to reflect the diversity of opinions and political views of its readership and is more accessible to those who wish to comment on issues of national and local concern. Therefore, while it may take an editorial stance which is political with a small or capital P, it is seldom fairly accused of bias. In fact it plays a vital local service by making the operations of local government and courts public and accountable, an important role in a democratic society.

Some aspiring journalists have great ambitions to get to a national and they would be disappointed if they didn't make it. Yet many journalists shun the nationals and choose to stay with a regional title because they feel they have a closer relationship with their readers and this is reflected in their coverage of the community. One editor of a major regional evening newspaper said:

You have to assume that you will always go anywhere at least twice so when writing a story about a person, or a place or an institution you have to feel that you've done that subject justice and you are perfectly happy to go back there. I suspect that's not always the case with the nationals.

While just about every town or region has its own newspaper, competition for jobs is still acute. But there is a myriad of ways in. For instance, some editors recruit through advertising or they may approach journalism colleges for likely candidates. As with the nationals, a reliable freelance stands a better chance of getting a job because they are known and trusted by the title. Also, impressive 'work experience' candidates are sometimes asked to stay and a good speculative letter of application can certainly prompt an interview.

Most large provincial towns have a regional morning or evening paper. The top-selling regional daily is the *London Evening Standard*, followed by the *Manchester Evening News*, *Wolverhampton Express and Star* and *Birmingham Evening Mail*. Scotland has a strong tradition of thriving regional dailies which reflect a Scottish emphasis on news and current affairs arguably lacking in many London-based dailies.

To give some indication of the extent of the regional newspaper industry, the Newspaper Society states that on a per issue basis, circulation of all regional and local newspapers in Great Britain totals over 53 million copies. By comparison, the circulation per issue of the national press averages around 30.5 million (September 1992). That means that around 90% of adults read a local or regional newspaper, nearly 30% more than a national.

In the regional and local sector, ownership is again fairly concentrated. Reed International is the largest owner of regional and local newspapers, publishing more than 100 weekly titles, closely followed by Thomson, United Newspapers, Pearson, EMAPP and Rothermere. The high cost of launching a new title – conservative estimates by the 1991 Sadler Inquiry suggest £10m – means that ownership is likely to remain concentrated for the distant future.

Tabloids and broadsheets

Newspapers today come in all shapes and sizes. Tabloid and broadsheet, local and national, newspapers vary not only in format but in the types of stories they contain. Broadsheet newspapers are large and give more room for stories to be written in greater detail. This format of newspaper tends to be associated with 'serious' reporting, with extensive coverage of international affairs and complicated issues at home. However, many tabloids, which are smaller and easier to handle, devote as much time and care to news but their stories may be written more concisely. One or two national tabloids concentrate on entertaining their readers with lighthearted stories and showbusiness gossip. It is a phenomenon almost unique to the UK that we will determine a newspaper's quality or authority in terms of its size. Many well-respected, investigative European newspapers are tabloid size simply because they are easier to handle. However, in the UK, journalists say there is a difference in the working experience of tabloid and broadsheet news people.

Tabloid reporters are under much more pressure from editors, proprietors and readers to seize upon the more sensational aspects of stories than their broadsheet counterparts. That is not to say that writing for a tabloid, with its punchy, concise language, upbeat news values and positive outlook, cannot be a fun and rewarding experience. Certainly the pay tends to be better and career prospects are very good. Broadsheet reporters must report stories in greater depth and devote more time to covering heavier national and international affairs which may not be touched upon in the tabloids.

While they are all called newspapers, they vary widely in terms of how much 'news' they contain. Editorial is only one of the many departments which work together to publish the paper. Ask three different readers which page they turn to first and you might receive three different replies; sport, advertising or television, for example. The news of the day might be low on the readers' list of priorities. Technological advances mean that radio and television are usually the first to deliver stories but newspapers have many other functions besides journalism. A local newspaper serves as a notice-board for the community as much as a mediator of current affairs. Job-hunters scour the pages of their evening title for opportunities while a company manager might turn to the business section of a national broadsheet to compare share prices. Commuters attempt the cryptic crossword to take their minds off work during their journey home. It takes a well co-ordinated team effort by all departments to bring the paper to the news-stand and to cater for the readers' varied interests.

THE STRUCTURE OF A NEWSPAPER

Basically, the organization of any newspaper office can be divided into three main departments: editorial, advertising and production.

- **Editorial** covers the research and writing of the main informational content of the newspaper including news, sport, features, specialist areas such as fashion and the television pages.

- **Advertising** deals with selling space in the newspaper for promotion and to contribute to the running cost of the newspaper.

- **Production** covers all the areas which lead to the actual construction and distribution of the newspaper.

You may be wondering where the photography department fits into the structure. It can fall into all three sections as this department gathers and creates images for both the editorial and advertising departments and will also work closely with the production department to ensure pictures and graphics generated are appropriate to their layouts in terms of size and content.

The bigger the newspaper operation, for example in the case of a major regional title or a national, the more 'sub-departments' there will be. Here the editorial department may be divided into sections dealing with business reporting, health, fashion and the arts whereas a reporter employed by a small local weekly newspaper would be required to write about a wide variety of topics. Similarly, a large title may subdivide its advertising department into classified, which covers birth announcements, for-sale notices and the like, and display, which deals with selling space to businesses.

All these functions in a newspaper require their own management but tend to be closely linked in the daily running of the title. The diagram opposite shows a typical structure of the organization of a newspaper with some of the job titles you might find within each department.

Whatever type or format of newspaper they work for, print journalists are often fiercely loyal to their medium while some see a spell on a newspaper as a stepping stone to radio or television. Those who want to stay in newspapers particularly enjoy writing and seeing their words in print.

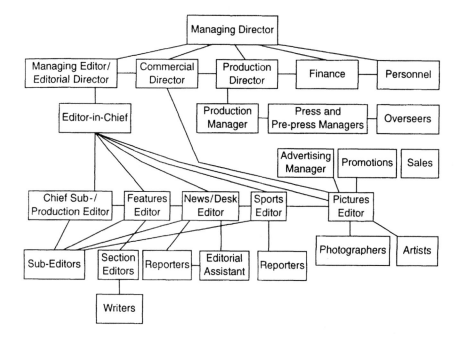

The structure of a newspaper's editorial department varies according to the size of the title and whether it is published daily or weekly. The Editor-in-Chief takes overall responsibility for their content of the newspaper and the way the pages are composed. Section leaders, such as the News Editor, Features Editor, Chief Sub-Editor and Pictures Editor are responsible to the Editor-in-Chief. The activities of the three main editorial sub-departments, News, Features and Sport will be described to give an insight into the work that goes into producing our daily newspapers.

News

News journalists generally see their role as to gather, summarize and mediate news of events and current affairs at home and abroad Their most important content is the 'hard' news of the day – that is, on a national paper for example, information about events and issues that will directly affect the lives of millions of readers, for instance, how the country is run, employment, housing and money. As a rule, and this is not a criticism of broadcast media which are limited by programme time constraints, news-papers are capable of reporting more diversely on most aspects of human action.

The scope of subjects reported upon in newspapers may be broader than broadcasts, but in terms of pressures and dead-lines, working as a general news reporter or on the newsdesk of, say, a major regional evening newspaper with hourly dead-lines is little different in many respects to working for hourly news programmes on the radio or television although the phys-ical mechanisms are different. Copy has to be written, updated, edited and subbed as it would be in broadcasting though print text will, for the most part, be more thorough than copy for broadcast.

There's no such thing as a breather in the newsroom of a busy paper. The newsdesk on a daily newspaper will be staffed for up to 20 hours a day, well into the early hours. Night news editors handle urgent news for the final editions. After one paper has gone to press, it's time to start working on the next one. And in the case of a regional evening newspaper, that can mean up to seven papers a day! News is highly complex and demands opti-mum organization. Therefore larger newsrooms tend to be divided up into a series of 'desks', including the newsdesk and sports desk, and staffed by specialists with an in-depth all-con-suming knowledge of their area.

The newsdesk is the real hub of the newsmaking process. Mission control, starbase alpha, however you look at it, this is where the news coverage of the day is commissioned and co-ordinated. One breakdown here and the whole operation is put into jeopardy.

News encompasses so many different aspects but is basically divided into home news, foreign news and specialist reporting, that is journalists employed to cover a specific area such as busi-ness or health. Most contributors to a national daily will tend to work under the direction of the Home News Desk. Staff and correspondents stationed abroad will report to the Foreign Editor who works closely alongside the News Editor.

At the start of each day, desk editors arrive to read through all the papers, press releases and wire service reports. They use their expertise to assess wire dispatches, stories running on from the previous day and news stories suggested by reporters and specialists to draw up the **news-list** – the list of issues and events to be covered in the next paper. It bears the likely details of the story plus reporters and photographers assigned to cover it.

Many stories, **diary** events such as court cases, press conferences, council meetings or government proceedings, can be planned in advance. But the unexpected occurrences such as bank raids and UFO landings are always welcomed and must be responded to immediately by ensuring there are enough reporters available to cover the story. Some stories are so massive, such as earthquakes or coups, that newsdesks will have to send reporters and photographers abroad at a moment's notice.

Depending upon the time of publication, a first news conference will normally take place mid-morning on a national daily, around 9am for a regional evening and mid-afternoon for a regional morning paper. In the case of a local weekly, the conference will be held formally once a week with further updating meetings. The times of these initial meetings are standard to most papers as they represent an opportunity for all the key players to meet and determine their actions for the day. The editor-in-chief presides over the conference with the various section editors covering news, features, pictures, sport, production and where applicable foreign and city, too. The expected stories to be included, the strengths and likely positioning in the paper are debated and a plan is drawn up. On a big national, a main conference will be held later in the day when copy has been pouring in and they can have a clearer idea of the overnight news agenda. Final decisions regarding content are made but there is also the possibility of an unexpected event overtaking at 9pm when the night editor will use his or her judgment as to whether the front page story or other major items should be moved or even replaced entirely. Around 75% of what is scheduled at the conference will go ahead as planned, but the night editor will be left occasionally with two or three possible front page leads to choose from.

How a story is covered

The reporter's first job of the day will be to 'do the calls'. That means telephoning all the local emergency services for details of crimes and other incidents of interest. If anything major has happened or is ongoing, they will inform their newsdesk which will decide whether a reporter should go to the scene with a photographer or cover the story from their desk.

Interviewing

Once assigned to cover a story, the journalist must interview eyewitnesses or others relevant to the issue or event. A newspaper journalist has many column centimetres to fill and must therefore carry out detailed interviews so that they have the fullest facts about the story. It is very frustrating to arrive back at the office and discover that you have not investigated each strand of the story in sufficient detail to produce enough copy. Most newspaper journalists work on the principle that it is far better to have too much information from which they can select the most pertinent facts. Traditionally journalists have to learn Teeline shorthand to a minimum speed of 100 wpm so that they can take fast, accurate notes. Now many reporters use portable mini cassette recorders as back-up. As the journalist prepares to write their copy, they must carefully read through their notes or transcription of their recorded interview and underline the most relevant information or interesting quotes. They will cross out any superfluous information. This method is particularly helpful if the reporter has to dictate their copy via telephone if they are on location and close to a deadline.

Filing

Many people want to go into reporting because they think it involves a lot of writing about issues of life-or-death significance. If that's you, you may be in for a shock. The writing and delivery of a news story is called **filing** and it is the part of the job that reporters have least time to devote to as most of their hours are spent researching and interviewing. A journalist may have pages of interviews and notes but only five minutes within which to file. That means writing and delivering, via a copytaker or computer.

Filing is done in a variety of ways. A few small papers which have not yet gone over to new technology still use typewriters where stories are literally bashed out onto sheets of A4 and subedited by hand.

Most newspapers now use wordprocessors and computers and no paper is used. These may be office-based or portable so that journalists can write their stories on a laptop, find a telephone socket and send their story digitally. However, many reporters rely on dictating their stories to copytakers in head office. That's fine if you are lucky enough to be given or lent a mobile 'phone but not so good if you have to race from a crowded courtroom to the village pub's phone with minutes to your deadline. Whatever way they do it, journalists usually have very little time to prepare their copy because they are busy getting the latest facts. This means they often have to file off the top of their heads. It sounds horrifying to the uninitiated but becomes easier with practice as you become accustomed to journalistic style. In fact often the best copy flows when you have to file spontaneously.

News writing

News writing is very different from the style used in literature which can frustrate some wordsmiths. News reporters must write in a style that is factual and concise, as space in newspapers is limited and expensive. There is no room for comment or ambiguity. Spelling, grammar and punctuation must also be impeccable. Feature writers and columnists have more scope for using language creatively.

In addition to researching, interviewing and filing copy, the reporter may also have to brief a photographer on what kind of picture they want and where and when it is to be shot. The story does not always finish when the journalists file. If they are working for a newspaper produced in several editions, they may need to update their copy every hour with the latest developments if it is an ongoing event such as a big fire. Over the next few days they will have to make sure they monitor the situation, checking, for instance, whether arrests have been made after a robbery, or whether the condition of a casualty has changed following a hit-and-run.

As well as responding to events, reporters must also initiate ideas for stories which means keeping in close touch with their contacts and checking council minutes, other media and even newsagents windows, where they can find interesting notices, for interesting ideas.

To give a better insight into how the reporting process is carried out, here is an example of how a fictional story about freak weather might be tackled by a daily morning newspaper on an hour-by-hour basis.

9am: News editor arrives at her desk to sift through mail, agency/ wire copy and checks broadcast news media. She was kept awake by the storms overnight and hears on the radio that villages have been put on flood alert as conditions are expected to worsen.

9.30am: The two early reporters arrive at the start of their eight-hour shifts and the news editor alerts them to the story. One (Sally) is sent out to areas at risk of flooding while the other (Steve) is asked to remain in the office and contact relevant agencies to see what is happening.

10am: Sally calls the news editor on her mobile telephone just before the first news conference to report that the river is about to burst its banks and nearby householders are being evacuated. She suggests sending a photographer to meet her. Meanwhile, Steve has been in touch with the Police, Fire, Ambulance and Army who have cancelled time off and are on full alert as the Meteorological Office has warned of more rain and gale force winds.

10.10am: The Editor-in-Chief holds his morning conference attended by the News Editor, Features Editor, Picture Editor, Sports Editor and Production Editor. They discuss the various prospects for the following day's edition and the News Editor reports that the worsening weather looks set to be a major story. The Picture Editor agrees to dispatch an extra photographer to the scene and the Features Editor suggests her department work on in-depth supporting articles which look into issues arising from severe weather. The Sports Editor says that one of the most important home matches for the local team may be rained off. The Production Editor and the Editor-in-Chief consider allocating a full page to the storms. Then the conference members discuss coverage of other major stories of the day.

Noon: Sally calls in to say that 20 homes have been evacuated and the school has been closed for the day. Steve has had a call from a freelance journalist who has interviewed a farmer who refuses to leave his animals. He passes the call to the News Editor who asks the freelance to file seven paragraphs 'on spec.'.

1pm: Steve has just spoken to a police press officer who says the river has burst its banks and flooded nearby streets and homes. The Fire Brigade are doing their best to contain the floods and are pumping water from houses. The Army are laying sandbags as flood defences. Steve begins to write an account of the early stages of the incident and how it is being tackled. It starts:

Emergency teams battled to save homes and businesses in storm-lashed Southby after the River Tern burst its banks. Twenty homes were evacuated and schoolchildren sent home as The Army joined forces with residents to lay sandbags as flood waters rose ...

Meanwhile, Sally has been interviewing evacuees who are being looked after by Salvation Army volunteers at the Church Hall. She files her first on-the-spot report of the day which she begins on a human interest note:

Worried villagers sang songs and told stories to keep up their spirits as they waited to hear what remained of their homes and livelihoods. The families were taking refuge in their Church Hall from rising flood waters, praying that the torrential rain would stop falling.

3pm: Calls come into the newsroom from worried villagers who say they have heard ambulance sirens. Steve contacts the local brigade who say they took two people to hospital after a road accident. He then telephones the Police, Fire Brigade and hospital for more details. Meanwhile, reports come in of further flooding and evacuation. The News Editor assigns another reporter, John, to the story, asking him to speak to the council to see what steps they are taking; to farmers, to see what damage has been done to crops; and to shopkeepers.

5pm: John has just taken a call from the local MP who is calling for the area to be declared a disaster zone and for Government funds to be sent in. Meanwhile the Features Department has produced two articles, one looking at the history of flooding in the region and another speculating on the long-term effects to the local economy.

5.15pm: The evening news conference. The scale of the incident is clearly greater than was anticipated that morning so three news pages are allocated for coverage plus one features page. The team discuss how the story should be angled for the following morning's paper, bearing in mind that the broadcast media will have covered the main details already. They decide to hinge their coverage on the potential long-term costs of the incident and how people will rebuild their lives as well as detailed accounts of the previous day's events. The Pictures Editor has an extensive collection of pictures from staff and freelance photographers and has photographs of eyewitnesses to go with Sally's interviews. The Production Editor asks the Pictures Editor to supply a computer-generated map of the disaster area.

6pm: Sally has interviewed the family of one of the injured motorists. They have lent her a photograph which she will deliver to the office. The water is subsiding and she reports on families rushing back to their homes to see the damage.

7pm: Steve and Sally can now go home and John, who is not due to finish until midnight, continues reporting. He telephones the emergency services, the Meteorological Office and other contacts for updates on the situation. Once the story is written, it will be read by the Night News Editor. If any alterations are needed, the story will be passed back to the reporter. If everything is in order, it will be sent electronically to the Chief Sub-Editor who will incorporate it into a page layout grid ready for production.

News: job descriptions

Here is a plan of how the news department might be organized followed by a description of some of the main roles.

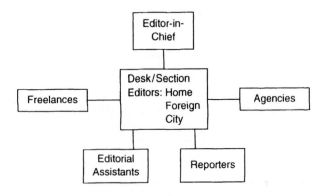

The editor-in-chief

Editor means different things according to what medium you are working in. In television, it can mean the person who physically packages the item ready for broadcast. In print there are a range of individuals who carry the term editor such as sub-editors, news editors and production editors. But it is the editor-in-chief who is responsible for the content of the publication and who is answerable for each edition of the newspaper in law.

Most editors these days tend to wear two hats – that of journalist and that of manager. Individuals will vary in terms of how much time they are able to devote to hands-on journalism. Some will physically decide what goes where on each page and will personally sub-edit the front page and write the leader. But for many, they must delegate these tasks to their deputies and assistants as they deal with the day-to-day management of vast numbers of journalists and a multi-million pound budget.

Case study: Editor, Liverpool Echo

This journalist worked for local and regional newspapers and agencies in Wales, the North West and Shropshire. He also worked as deputy editor of *The Journal* in Newcastle before becoming Editor of the Echo's sister morning paper, the *Daily Post,* later moving to the evening title.

You are half a journalist and half a manager. As a manager, I am in charge of a multi-million pound budget, 80-odd staff and all the problems that come with that. As a journalist I am in charge of a daily product that you are always wanting to make as good as you can from the front page to the back. Those two roles don't always fit very neatly. That is why bringing out newspapers is a team business rather than an individual business. Though I do think it's important for every newspaper to have some sort of individual stamp to it or else it doesn't have a personality.

There is no such thing as a typical day. I start at 7am, go through the papers, read our early pages and try to get a feel of what's happening. Most of my day until 2pm is driven by that day's newspaper. The afternoons tend to be spent catching up with what's in the mail, planning for tomorrow and the weeks ahead and trying to fit in the managerial role. A lot of editors are directors of the company they work for because the company feels, quite rightly, that the editor's voice should be heard around board table. So all of that adds to the general workload. Direct journalist jobs on a regular basis include running the morning news conference, to give editorial direction to the paper. I like to write the leading articles and do it as many days as I can. I want to be involved in Page One, either helping to design it or helping to sub it or determining what the main splash headlines are going to be. As each production cycle comes to an end, I'll prowl around on the stone [platform where pages are composed before printing] and check pages. The fun of the job is the journalistic part and I'd hate to lose track of that.

Desk/section editors

Working to the editor-in-chief are these senior journalists who organize reporters and act as the link between the newsroom, editors, sub-editors, photographers and, of course, the outside world. Some will be in charge of news while others will coordinate features, sport and all the other sections too. As experienced journalists, section editors have a judgmental role, sifting through all the possible stories to decide what should be covered and how. They brief reporters on stories and make suggestions as to picture coverage and set a deadline. Throughout their reporting, particularly if they are sent out of the office, the reporter will maintain close contact with the newsdesk to update them on developments and to receive advice on how to pursue the story.

Copytasters

News agencies feed their stories directly into the papers' computer networks so they can be pulled up on screen. This material coupled with copy filed by staffers via the newsdesk is sifted through by the copytasters who select the items to be used in the paper that day. This role is undertaken by experienced journalists, sometimes the chief sub-editor or deputy editor, who act as the gatekeepers of the newsmaking process, determining what stories should be considered for inclusion and which can be omitted. Their decisions will largely depend upon the type of newspaper, the readership and the amount of available space. A national tabloid, for instance, may have very little space available. Its space is more likely to be devoted to domestic exclusives from their own staff rather than international stories from wire agencies or mundane court cases from the regions. Copytasters on regional morning papers, on the other hand, will use their experience and news sense to determine what their readers will want to see and are more likely to be interested in stories that are relevant to their local audience's lives. These may include council decisions, the outcome of court cases and general interest articles about community groups which would not be considered by a national paper. Copytasters, therefore, need to know their newspaper intimately and understand its market and readership appeal.

News agency, or wire copy, is sifted through, but priority is always given to what the paper's own staffers write. Oniy a tenth of agency copy submitted might get used.

Editorial assistant

It's a well-known fact that many top executives could not function without their assistant. In newsrooms this is definitely the case. Though it sounds patronizing – and it really isn't meant to – the editorial assistant is an indispensable feature of most news organizations. Their role is, basically, to ensure the smooth operation of the newsmaking process. Their first job of the day is to process all the mail that comes into the office and ensure that everything reaches the right person. Any important dates will be inserted into the news diary and press releases and letters will be filed. Throughout the day, in between answering calls and queries, they will act as a liaison between news and other departments such as advertising and photography. A vital part of their job is to maintain cuttings and contacts files, an invaluable resource to the newsroom when information is needed swiftly. In smaller newsrooms which do not have a separate library, the editorial assistant may also run the picture archive, cataloguing and supplying prints on request to the production department. They may also contribute copy for the publication or assist with editing when required. Administrative duties are an important feature of the job so wordprocessing or typing and shorthand skills are useful.

Journalists happily admit the editorial assistant knows every-one's jobs inside out and without them the finely tuned system would practically collapse. There is no doubt that the job is demanding, requiring a great deal of energy and the patience of a saint – the editorial assistant is often on the frontline when it comes to dealing with the public.

It is a career in its own right and while it may be a route into reporting, the role should not be viewed so simplistically. Successful, motivated editorial assistants are well-placed to work their way up the ladder, and not only because they hear about vacancies first. While people hoping to enter the industry at reporter or editor level may be well qualified on paper, they frequently lack the basic news sense and good organization skills of the experienced editorial assistants.

News reporters

There are two types of news reporters, general and specialist. General reporters write about a wide range of events and issues while specialist journalists, like crime reporters, science corre-spondents or political staff, concentrate on their own areas of expertise. Many papers also employ columnists who describe news events and issues from their personal and subjective point of view as opposed to the unbiased approach traditionally adopted by hard news reporters. This role will be covered in more depth in the features section.

General news reporters As their title suggests, they literally have to turn their hand to anything, from crime stories to council meet-ings. News reporters' jobs are so diverse it is hard to provide a job description. Their role will vary depending on what kind of paper they work for. On a local weekly, they could end up report-ing, laying out pages and taking photographs one day and the next they may end up deputizing for the editor at a high-level business launch.

On larger publications, with larger staffs, their role will be more clear-cut. They have a remit to initiate ideas for hard news stories of general interest as well as work to briefings by their newsdesk. Usually based in the head office of the news-paper, they will tend to operate on a shift basis. On an evening regional paper, reporters will arrive at 7am, 8am, 10am and will work at least eight hours, five or six days a week. On a morning paper, they will start later in the day and may end up working till 3am. It can be frustrating that not everything a journalist writes is destined for the front-page splash. A lot of time is spent writing fillers – one paragraph 'news-in-brief' type reports – or having their stories rejected. A story may seem the obvious splash at 10am but by 4.40pm a new and better story has come along which relegates your hard work to page 27.

Specialist reporter Specialists tend to be employed by larger papers to write about a particular topic of which they have expert knowledge. In addition to their expertise in their field, specialist reporters need all of the attributes and skills of a general reporter including good interview techniques, writing flair and the ability to make their subject relevant and interesting to the readership. The arts, health, politics and science are key specialisms which usually require the journalist to have a qualification or other attribute that illustrates their expertise and authority. Crime reporters will often be dedicated to that role because they need to spend time building up rapports with agencies such as the courts and police as well as communities to bring the stories behind the headlines.

At one time, you could not pick up a newspaper without seeing an environmental story on the front page. From the ozone layer to the tropical rainforests to the dolphin, they were attention-grabbing stories that have motivated the average person in the street to do something about the planet. But it was clearly a trend. One environment correspondent said he rarely does much these days. 'The environment has gone out of fashion,' he said. 'I hope it comes back!'

National broadsheets often devote a whole department and several daily pages to covering business and finance, labelled under the overall umbrella term of City. Activities in the Stock Market and financial world are dealt with in detail along with foreign markets. There is also coverage of banking, markets, commodity prices, stocks and share prices, mining, oil and energy, exchange rates and so on. The City Desk and writers must obviously be specialists with an expert knowledge of the mechanisms of the world of finance and commerce.

Case study: Media Correspondent, The Guardian

It's 8pm in *The Guardian's* London newsroom and the finishing touches are being put to the front page lead. On such a major national daily, you would imagine all hell to be breaking loose, editors shouting down telephones, reporters bashing computers. Not the case here. You can barely hear the click of a keyboard. Someone switches up the volume of the television news on a set in the corner. 'Turn it down a bit, mate,' is the appeal from the hushed newsdesk. And by ten past that's it. Another edition is on its digital journey to the presses at the Isle of Dogs.

This calm, well-planned approach is typical of most deadlines in today's sophisticated daily newsrooms. *The Guardian* sets deadlines for its pages throughout the day so there is a constant stream of news coming in. Reporters work on a shift basis, starting at 10.30am, with the final shift ending at 2am the following morning. Pressure mounts between 6pm and 8pm, then the operation is handed over to the night news editors and two reporters for any last minute coverage of big stories.

This journalist began his professional journalism career as a trainee with the *East Anglian Daily Times,* a morning regional newspaper. He gained his Proficiency Certificate and stayed with the title for five years until he eventually became news editor. In 1989, he joined *The Guardian* as a reporter for one year, rapidly progressing to the newsdesk. After two years on the desk, staff were reshuffled and he became media correspondent.

'I was very happy to take up the challenge and it is a good job,' he said. 'Various specialist areas seem to come in and out of fashion. At the moment there is tremendous interest in the media and all broadsheets have a media correspondent.'

While the term correspondent may conjure up an image of a maverick foreign reporter living out of a holdall and using crackly lines to transmit stories from far-flung places, the word is in fact meaningless. Correspondent can just be another term for reporter but is particularly favoured on broadsheets where it carries more authority.

His remit is to provide copy for *The Guardian*'s dedicated weekly media supplement, co-ordinated by a media editor, but he also provides many column inches to the daily general news pages and works to the instruction of the general newsdesk. The type of story he covers varies greatly, from showbusiness-oriented features to in-depth analysis of issues surrounding press freedom, broadcasting Acts, White Papers and political or business matters affecting the media.

'That's part of the media's appeal – it can lighten a somewhat serious paper but also provide some very meaty copy,' he said.

His day is never the same:

My working day normally starts at home with reading, or rather skimming, several newspapers. Depending on my diary, I'll get to the office between 9.30 and 10am. I might have a press conference to attend in the morning, such as the launch of a network's Autumn programming. It may not yield a particularly good story but it does give me the chance to meet press officers and other contacts who can help me generate stories. You do have to get out of the office and we are lucky being in central London that we can get to most places easily. There is no way you should do all your research over the telephone.

At lunchtime, I may meet up with a colleague or another contact. Most of my copy goes on the inside pages so I need to file my pieces in the early afternoon. They are written on a terminal which is part of an Atex computer system which allows me to follow my story's progress from when I have written it, to the newsdesk, then to the sub-editors and beyond. I may have other interviews or stories to write in the afternoon and get away from the office early evening. But my day varies greatly. For instance, when the BBC White Paper came out, I started at 8.30am, went to two press briefings, came back to write umpteen stories for 1pm, then another press conference in the afternoon, then more writing. And it can be very unpredictable. Yesterday it was very quiet then, all of a sudden, the telephone rang at 6pm with the announcement that *The Oldie* (a high-profile magazine) had closed.

> You can't just switch off when you get home. I remember when the bombs went off in the City after the 1992 General Election. I heard the blasts at home and went straight into the office and started working. I get calls on a Sunday and at midnight as everyone does. When big things happen like Thatcher's resignation, I feel privileged to be at the centre of things. But those events tend to stick in your mind as most days are fairly routine.
>
> He said there are many benefits to working for a national title:
>
> People do actually hold you in some regard and will return your calls, which came as quite a shock after working on a regional daily. We are regarded as important and there is no problem in gaining access to high-powered figures in the media. They want to talk to us. But I'm not blasé, I still get a great buzz when I walk through the front door each day.

So the working life of news journalists is hectic, pressured and very exhilarating. But it takes more than news to fill a paper and there are many other types of journalists working in print. There is no doubt that as radio and television might be many people's first source of news, papers have to look to other ways of attracting readers. Expanding the features side is the approach most newspapers have taken. Feature writers, for instance, bring greater depth and analysis to the factual coverage provided by their news counterparts as well as creating the leisure and entertainment-based sections of the newspaper.

Features

Feature pages usually fall in the middle of a paper or in separate sections. They provide in-depth coverage on a wide range of subjects from topical news issues to entertainment, health, education, the environment, human interest, fashion, music and the arts. Some of the feature pages are prepared ahead of the news pages but their topic must be current. As one features editor explains, newspapers provide a different service to the type of coverage given by periodicals: 'A magazine, by it's very nature, has a long shelf-life so you can pick it up in a dentist's waiting room three months after publication while you are waiting for your filling and it still means something to you. With a lot of magazines, the March issue will be produced the December before. We try to be more topical and reactive to things that are happening now.' Therefore, much of the content of newspaper features sections is as up-to-the-minute and as reactive to events as the news pages. Some papers will include upwards of 80 features pages a week, including supplements; more if you consider colour magazine inserts.

What is the difference between news and features?

Some people would describe features as a long news story but it's more than that. It's the opportunity for a writer to put more of themselves into what they are writing rather than just facts in order of importance. If we take the example of the flood story, news journalists will report the facts of the story, that is, they will write an account of what happened, who, what, why, where, when, how, and speak to the people involved and affected. A feature writer tackling the same story will look at the issue in more depth than just providing instant facts. They will want to ask, for example, if more could have been done to prevent the river bursting its banks and flooding homes. They might look in detail at insurance cover and how householders will try to rebuild their lives. The features section is also entertainment oriented and, as one features editor puts it, 'It's an oasis in the paper to give you a smile and make you stop and pause for thought. It's something out of the ordinary.' Celebrity gossip, television and film news, fashion, music, crosswords and weather reports all go to make up lively relief from the hard news of the day.

Features: job descriptions

The structures and size of features departments varies according to the size of the newspaper. Some national titles will have several tiers of staff with their features department being subdivided further into sections, whereas a local weekly may require its news reporters also to write features. Some regional newspapers operate a flexible system whereby its own news reporters can

contribute features on a freelance basis for which they are paid
extra. This diagram gives a basic plan of a features department,
followed by a description of some of the key roles.

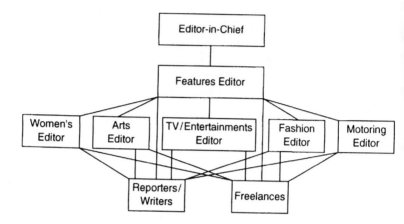

Features editors

This person is responsible for the entire section and works to the
editor-in-chief with whom they will meet daily. Unlike news,
feature pages can be planned days, weeks or even months ahead
and features editors must continually generate ideas for new
material.

A features editor will have several years' experience in news
before moving into features as the material they deal with can
range from current affairs comment and analysis to lighthearted
leisure. The feature editor's day will usually start by meeting the
editor-in-chief at the daily conference to discuss coverage of the
topical issues of the day. The features editor will describe how they
plan to fill their section to see whether other department heads
think they are good ideas. This is also an opportunity for this
person to liaise with the pictures editor to obtain photographic
coverage for that day's features pages and the news editor whose
account of the day's top stories may inspire new pieces.

Once the day's agenda has been discussed, the features editor
will meet with their section editors who may include the arts
editor, women's editor, motoring editor and TV editor, depending on the individual newspaper. At this meeting, prospective

feature ideas will be considered in detail along with budgetary considerations such as the amount of photographs to be taken, travel expenses and the cost of commissioning freelance writers. The features editor will manage the department's resources and must budget for a variety of expenses, from bus fares to the theatre to catering for over-dinner interviews with film stars! In addition to managing their department, most features editors take a hands-on role and write pieces for inclusion in the newspaper.

Section editors
These people may have a designated page or pages to fill daily or weekly. They usually have a dual role both as writers and as commissioning editors. As writers, they will have an in-depth knowledge of their specific area. As commissioning editors, their role is to generate ideas for their section and ask either staff or freelance journalists to produce pieces to their specification. With the exception of motoring and the arts, feature specialisms are non-technical and section editors often specialize through choice rather than as a result of prior training as their skill lies in idea generation and understanding what their readers want.

Feature writers
Staff feature writers tend to be generalists; that is they will write on a host of topics. One day, they might be road-testing a new car, the next writing about prams. If the paper needs a specialist they will tend to commission an outside expert to write the feature. The daily work of a feature writer is not dissimilar to that of a news journalist. They must both suggest ideas for pieces as well as respond to briefs issued by their editors, they must carry out research and interview by telephone and face-to-face and they must then write their article in an appropriate style for the newspaper to a deadline. It is therefore rare – but not unknown so don't be discouraged – to work in features without having a news background. However, feature writing is different from reporting in that journalists in features employ their writing skills to a greater extent than in news. You need to be able to paint a mental picture of a scene for someone who wasn't there. In addition, whereas a news journalist might report on several stories in a day, the feature writer will usually have to produce

lengthier pieces which require greater research and longer inter-views. So they may take a couple of days to complete one article. But news sense and reporting skills are vital to gain information in the first place and to know how to angle the copy to grab the readers' attention.

Feature writers tend to have a 'closer' relationships with the reader in that they may become known for their views, which have to be kept out of straight news reporting. They may also describe their own experiences or write far more personally, putting their feelings and emotions into their piece. There is a fair amount of scope for contributing freelance features to news-papers as editors who commission work from staff and outside contributors will be the first to admit that thinking up new, stim-ulating ideas is the hardest part of their job.

Features sub-editors

Features departments have dedicated sub-editors. This role will often be undertaken by the section editors and features editor as the separation of duties between roles tend to be more blurred in this department. Sub-editors working in features lay out and edit pages in a more flexible style than in news, making more creative use of pictures and typography than would normally be permis-sible on hard news pages. As well as the content being light relief from the rigours of the news pages, the brighter or more dramatic appearance of features offer relief and stimulation to the eye.

Specialists

There are journalists dedicated to covering specific areas on many larger newspapers. These areas include the arts, motoring, television and cinema, comment and fashion. Let us look at these latter two areas in more depth.

Comment and opinion Another part of the newspaper which tends to fall under the category of features is comment. In its many forms, comment is the heart of a newspaper, revealing the publi-cation's identity, character and broad political standpoint. As well as reporting news as objectively as they can, newspapers like to pass opinion on the events and issues of the day. Unlike broadcast news media, which often have to remain impartial by law, newspapers are at liberty to express their views which can often endear them to their readership – or provoke angry objection. The reader tends to have a more intimate relationship with a newspaper because of its role in stimulating discussion and opinion.

Comment and opinion always tend to be clearly demarcated from the factual news reporting of the edition which always endeavours to be objective. Comment will be carried in various forms:

- editorials/leaders written to put across the paper's standpoint on a topic of the day;

- cartoons;

- reader's letters;

- personal columns by staff journalists or others invited to express their opinion.

To be asked by your paper to write a column is quite an honour and one which is usually only bestowed on those whose views will evoke a reaction from the reader. A staff journalist may be picked because of their sense of humour or particularly good arguments or turn of phrase. Celebrities with whom readers can emphathize, politicians, sports people or others with an interesting view on the world may also be asked to be guest columnists.

One writer on a daily morning regional title says:

> I do a weekly column on Monday of 600 to 700 words usually split into three items. Although 700 words doesn't sound very much, in newspaper terms it is quite a chunk. It demands greater concentration on the part of the reader so it's got to be quite lively and creative. I try to take a news event and twist it into a personalized form, and attempt to make it sympathetic to the people in the story. I also feel that quite a lot of trivial events can be told well and be made more interesting than major events. The column is the opportunity to tell the story in a different way, not constrained by the discipline of balance.

Some columnists deliberately adopt a strong or controversial view to provoke a reaction from the reader.

Fashion writing We have all watched with amazement television documentaries about the world of fashion and seen the fashion editors of glossy magazines sipping champagne as they watch lithe models glide down the catwalks of the world's most beautiful cities. But did you know that the average working day of a fashion writer involves begging store managers to lend them clothes for a photo shoot, carting heavy bundles of coats, dresses and shoes from one studio to another then back to the shop, booking models, briefing photographers and, at the end of the long day, looking more like Cruella de Ville than Claudia Schiffer? Both sides to the job are very much exaggerated but the latter version is closer to the truth for the majority of people working in fashion journalism on newspapers and magazines.

There is a difference between working for the fashion and style pages of a newspaper and the pages of a glossy magazine. Newspaper fashion pages are usually text-dominated while magazines have more scope to feature page after page of sumptuous images and comparatively little text. On a magazine, fashion pages can be planned up to six months ahead and have far more visual impact and influence on the buying trends of the public than a newspaper's. This is because magazines are aiming themselves at a clearly demarcated audience with the result that outfits are selected and pages stylized to appeal to their readers. Magazines have the resources and authority, through the patronage of advertising from the major fashion houses, to hire top models and photographers and scour the season's shows to present the very latest designs in the most appealing ways. Many magazines are sold on their fashion content and reputation alone and are in stiff competition with similar titles to be the first to feature the latest designs. Journalists working for these publications will aspire to foster a good relationship with fashion houses so that they are guaranteed good seats at fashion shows and possibly a sneak preview of some of the designers' latest creations. Additionally, newspapers have a broader readership profile than magazines so the fashion featured must have widespread appeal with outfits aimed for a range of incomes and age-groups.

Anyone who has flicked through fashion pages will realize that the text accompanying the pictures has a unique style quite unlike that of news or even features. Newspaper fashion is in many cases written factually. The feature may hinge around the work of a successful rising star in the design world or the opening of a new clothing emporium. Alternatively, the story may be made into hard news by covering the furore over a controversially revealing catwalk collection! This type of copy will be structured in a similar way to news and will contain quotes and factual background material. Magazine writing style is very different. This is because magazines are more leisure-oriented than newspapers and do not have the same factual and up-to-the-minute emphasis as newspapers. Magazine journalists explore language to conjure up a mood or atmosphere. They attempt to transport the reader on a journey to an exotic location with the clothing to match, or they will create a scenario such as a job interview or first date and depict suggestions for appropriate dress. Atmospheric adjectives and adverbs are sprinkled liberally to enhance the aspirational aspect to the feature. As pictures tend to dominate, text in magazines is kept to a minimum and is sometimes restricted to a brief introduction and short description of the clothing, price and stockists on each page.

Many aspects of the work of fashion writers for newspapers and magazines are similar:

1. organizing models, photographers, locations;
2. directing the fashion shoot;
3. selecting and editing pictures;
4. writing copy and headlines;
5. going to fashion shows and keeping ahead of the latest trends.

Whereas magazines have large teams of fashion journalists, newspapers may have only one dedicated fashion reporter who may also double up as a feature writer or woman's editor. Pressure of time and resources means newspapers are unlikely to produce many of their own shoots. Instead, they will obtain pictures of catwalk collections from agencies or will use photos sent in by fashion houses and stores.

Writing ability coupled with visual flair are essential attributes for the fashion journalist. You need to demonstrate a passion for clothes and be prepared to work very long hours in pursuit of the finished pages. On a regional paper, which may have a women's or fashion supplement or produce an advertising feature on clothes, fashion journalists can work till all hours in a sweaty studio but the overriding ambition that you will eventually find your way into a national glossy magazine and go on shoots to far-flung corners of the world will keep you going. But top fashion editors will tell you that even that is no picnic as the best light for photographing models is often at 4am!

In addition to news and features, sport has a dedicated place in a newspaper.

Sport

Sports coverage plays a major role in a newspaper's function and, with burgeoning competition from broadcast media and the vast array of new sports magazines entering the market, papers are having to work very hard to keep readers and advertisers interested in their product. A large proportion of readers are fans of one sport of another and will be fans of certain teams and performers, whether the reader is an avid spectator who wants to relive the experience through a review, or simply an armchair enthusiast. The kudos of association with major, prestigious sporting events which are seen through the eyes of the newspaper makes the organization seem responsive to readers' needs. Readers expect build-up, match reports and in-depth articles about the personalities involved. A sign of this is the production of regional editions of national newspapers to cater for different areas of the country and their corresponding affiliations. Further proof of the significance of sports coverage is the corresponding interest from related advertisers (including companies involved with the sport such as clubs, equipment manufacturers and sport information telephone-line operators) and general advertisers wanting to reach sports fans (such as insurance firms).

While newspapers cannot provide live coverage like their broadcast counterparts, they have a special and unique role by offering in-depth reporting of events in a reflective mode. Newspapers have more scope for analysis and can often devote several pages or a pull-out supplement whereas radio and television in sports coverage does not always have the same analytical scope.

Which sports are covered?

Traditionally, those sports which are most enshrined in the British way of life are given greatest coverage. This includes football, rugby, cricket, tennis, boxing and athletics. These sports draw in the biggest crowds and inspire major reader emotion and feedback. Correspondingly, massive amounts of money are involved in terms of sponsorship and advertising. It is often argued that there is a parallel lack of coverage of other sports. Sports editors claim they must evaluate a variety of factors in determining what they can include such as availability of space and reader demand. The types of sports covered also varies from title to title. Whereas tabloids lend more space to big-name sports, including boxing, horse-racing and American football, the broadsheets write stories about activities such as cycling and hockey. The tabloid press is also very interested in the personalities who take part. There are added regional variations in the amount of space devoted to specific sports to reflect the character and tradition of the local community. For example, rugby league is important in Warrington and rowing in Henley.

Sport always has a defined position in every newspaper so the reader can instantly find the section. In tabloids, for example, it is traditionally the back pages. But an indication of sport's importance in the media is that stories involving our sporting heroes frequently receive headline coverage on the front pages. Even a top tennis player's new haircut will find its way into the news or features section. Just as sport plays a powerful part in the media and society, the media has tremendous power over the sporting industry as exemplified by managers being put under pressure to quit due to public concern articulated through the pages of newspapers.

The layout and content of sports pages

Just as in the rest of the newspaper, the sports pages are designed in a way that is attention-grabbing and gripping to keep the reader interested. Often there is scope for injecting humour into the language of headlines and in the choice of pictures. Colourful, action shots are used in a large size to heighten impact with readers who are used to television coverage of an event. Accompanying the match reports and stories are results tables, league charts and, like other sections of the newspaper, a sports columnist will have their say about the 'state of the game' and personalities involved.

How a sports reporter covers a football match

If they are covering the local team, the journalist will concentrate on their performance, even if they have had a heavy defeat, putting it in the context of previous games and future fixtures. If less partisanship is required, in the case of a national for instance, the reporter will concentrate upon the winning team's performance.

The style of coverage will depend upon factors including the amount of time, available space, the importance attached to the game or the result and in part the writer's style.

At the ground, the journalist gains entry via a pass provided by the club or a ticket to the press box which is normally situated in the ground's main stand in a central position. This is an enclosed area for exclusive use by the media, containing plug-in points for radio broadcast equipment, telephone sockets and power points for laptop computers.

The writer aims to arrive in good time to pick up last-minute team news, to trade gossip with colleagues and check any interesting pre-match statistics such as whether a player is approaching a goal-milestone as this can be incorporated into the introduction to the report. Equipment also has to be prepared, if only a stopwatch, notebook, pens and programme.

Although methods and styles differ from reporter to reporter, during the game the journalists will note the time and the players involved in any important action, such as whose pass set another free to shoot or who made an important cross or save. Corners, bookings and crowd attendance are also noted. The record of the game will be divided into two halves with a separate section for each team.

As the game nears its end, the sports reporter starts collating their information and composing an introduction to their piece emphasizing what they see as the most important elements to be drawn from the game's outcome, allowing for any last-minute developments. These elements might include possible relegation to a lower division or qualification to the next round of a cup competition. Alternatively, if the reporter has enough time before their deadline, a post-match dispute or comments by the manager could provide the vital angle for longer reports. Their report might start:

Paul Gascoigne capped his return to the England team with a dazzling two-goal performance against Germany at Wembley last night.

And England boss Terry Venables revealed he almost didn't field the influential playmaker following his comeback from injury. Venables said: '.......'

After the introduction and qualifying sentences are written, the game's high-points are reviewed though not necessarily in chronological order. The journalist must always take into the account the audience and newspaper they are writing for and use appropriate language.

Sports reporters with tight deadlines will read their reports over the telephone to copytakers in the newspaper office or send them down telephone lines from their laptop computers moments after final whistle. Journalists working for a team's local papers are expected to provide supplementary articles such as an interview with a player who has performed well, the opposition manager's thoughts of the local team, and so on. These will be positioned on the inside back pages with an article on the back page giving an overall review to act as a summary and 'taster' for the material within.

Sports journalism: job descriptions

Coverage is centred around the sports desk which is a separate entity from the newsdesk and has its own budget. The sports editor oversees a team of reporters and sub-editors dedicated to the subject. Senior reporters can lay out pages as well as write. There is further specialization within the team in that there are dedicated soccer writers, cricket correspondents and racing reporters. In areas which are home to, say, several top soccer teams, individual reporters often devote their time to reporting one specific club for continuity's sake. The staff team is backed up by a list of contributors who submit copy on a freelance basis. Round-ups and results are also supplied by sports and news agencies locally, nationally and internationally.

This sports desk structure will vary from title to title depending upon resources. For example, a weekly free distribution newspaper may have one sports staff member who combines the roles of editor, writer and sub. At the other end of the scale, a national newspaper will have a sports desk based in London with a satellite desk in its regional offices in Manchester and Glasgow. That's the overall picture; now let us look at the key players more closely.

Sports editor
This person has a dual role in terms of managing resources and overseeing the editorial process. They have a limit on how

much they can spend on copy from freelance contributors so they will try to achieve as much coverage of the main events at optimum cost. However, the bigger newspapers invest a great deal in their sports coverage because of the prestige and knock-on news stories it brings. As well as the monetary constraints, there are considerations about fitting the available space. Major editorial decisions therefore have to be made about what to include and exclude which takes considerable journalistic maturity as there is the risk of alienating readers. This means that sports editors have to combine expertise as a journalist with unshakeable judgment over what their audience wants to read. They have usually worked their way to the top of their profession following time as a general news reporter before breaking into sport.

Sports reporters
Journalists who are dedicated to writing about sport vary in their role according to the title they work for. A sports reporter on a local weekly might have to operate single-handedly, covering matches, editing freelance copy and even lay out pages. By contrast, on bigger newspapers they can specialize to cover one specific sport and may even dedicate their work to reporting one particular club. Among their duties are attending matches and writing reports. They must keep as much contact with clubs as possible during the week before a game. This provides important material for so-called build-up articles of which a daily newspaper runs one every day on a big club or prior to a big game. One day, such an article might consist of an interview with a star player; the next, a youngster who's just broken through the ranks for his first big match; another day the opinions of a former player now playing for the opposing side. For the local media particularly, all these build-up articles are expected to have a good local angle and be exclusive because readers expect the best sports coverage from this sector as the newspaper co-exists in the same community as the club.

Sports reporters must be first with the latest transfer and injury news and this is achieved by maintaining good, regular contact with the manager, the players themselves and anyone close to them, such as the editor of the match programmes.

The personal attributes essential to sports journalism are largely the same as in any other field of journalism. They have to be quick-thinking and a good listener. They must have the ability to ask questions that readers and fans want answered. Sports journalists must be able to mix well with colleagues from other media organizations and get on with sports people. To do this, they have to cope under pressure and really know what they are talking about. Flexibility is vital as sports reporters have to work long hours late into the evening and at weekends. There is a lot of waiting around and some work is done outdoors in all conditions.

Entry into sports journalism is similar to other fields of journalism. Most reporters start on a local level either on a work experience or freelance basis submitting articles to the sports editor to demonstrate their talent. A specialist knowledge about a major sport is a great help if not essential. It is worth applying for general news jobs as a route into sports for two reasons; firstly, the writing and research skills learned in news journalism are helpful in sport and, secondly, news reporters with a proven interest can often move across into sport if an opportunity arises. The qualifications required to be a sports journalist are the same as in other fields of journalism depending upon the route of training or entry.

Sports sub-editors
A great deal of the information about sports reporters also applies to sub-editors who may perform reporting duties in addition to laying out pages. The work of the sports sub involves designing the overall page, checking and editing reporters' copy to fit the available space, writing appropriate headlines, selecting and fitting pictures into the layout. As most newspapers now use colour on their sports pages for its eye-enhancing immediacy, the sub-editor must be skilled in the use of colour and the psychological effect it has upon the reader. Sports sub-editors need an in-depth knowledge about sport to help them write appropriately witty headlines and to understand the significance of the story.

Sports photographers
Smaller newspapers use the services of staff and freelance photographers who cover sport as well as general news and are basically good all-rounders, rather than dedicated sports photographers. It is only the bigger papers and large agencies who can afford to employ specialists. They must have a knowledge of the sport they are covering in order to capture the right moment. They must be able to recognize key players and potential situations. They must have technical expertise because they work

with variable lighting in poor conditions capturing fast-moving action. This is with the added challenge of using colour which most newspapers rely upon for their sports pictures.

With so many media competing for pictures of the stars, the photographer must build up the trust of players and managers to allow him or her access to behind the scenes shots.

Syndication

Not everything you read in a newspaper has been produced by staff or freelance journalists working for that title. Horoscopes, crosswords, cartoons and even problem pages are frequently syndicated. This means they are produced by an agency to which the title can subscribe. The agency will not only supply the text but accompanying photographs and graphics if required. Some agencies will 'wire' the information so that it appears as a paper print-out ready to be pasted up on the page for production. But as many pages are laid out on-screen, the information can be sent down a telephone line to the newspaper's computer network where it will be stored as a file which can be retrieved by a sub-editor as they compose their page.

Newspaper pictures

Imagine how dull newspapers would be without photographs. Pictures not only illustrate the people or places mentioned in the stories, they serve a vital role in bringing visual relief to the pages which would otherwise be covered in grey text. A picture can be news in its own right by portraying situations or evoking feelings which cannot be expressed through words. Images of the effects of famine or war are a case in point. These kind of pictures need few accompanying words to convey the message. Whether the photograph makes you feel happy or sad, satisfied or angry, you can be sure a great deal of work has gone into putting that picture on the page.

What makes a good newspaper photograph?

For every single photograph published, dozens are rejected. This picture-editing process is performed on several levels –

by photographers as they print their images and decide which to submit, by the picture editor who selects which to pass to the newsdesk and by the sub-editor who decides whether to incorporate the image in the layout. Factors influencing choice include how well the photograph illustrates and supports the text, and its general composition, that is what is in the picture, and its tonal quality. For example, a grey-looking picture with insufficient black and white elements will not reproduce well. If the people depicted have inappropriate facial expressions or are facing in the wrong direction, the picture may be cast aside.

Colour and black-and-white

An increasing number of newspapers are harnessing colour for its visual impact and apparent realism. While colour images are far more expensive to produce and reproduce than black-and-white, no expense is spared when it comes to competing with rival titles and winning the circulation war. However, other newspapers, including leading broadsheets have rejected colour believing black-and-white pictures to have greater drama and impact. The reader has to use their imagination to supplement the lack of hue. Whatever format is used, working in black-and-white or colour both carry their challenges. The photographer working in black-and-white must visualize the scene in shades of grey. When working with colour, the photographer must be sensitive to shifts in tonal intensity and the effects lighting will have on the finished result. Even when they have mastered this most complex skill they still have to address what composition is going to work well on the printed page.

The practice of press photography

Presiding over the picture desk is the picture editor or chief photographer who has the job of overseeing image-gathering and briefing his or her team of staff and freelance photographers and often a darkroom assistant too. When a photograph is accompanying a story, the newsdesk or individual reporters fill out a picture request form with a synopsis of the story time, date and location and the time the processed picture is required. The picture editor keeps check on the whereabouts of the available photographers who divide their time between being on the road in cars linked to the picture desk by radio and in the studio or darkroom. If the picture editor is managing a tight budget, certain picture requests may be refused. This can happen at night or weekends when staffing levels are lower and the photograph has only a slim chance of being used or the subject is unlikely to be photogenic. News photographs don't always come from staff or freelance sources. Agencies operating locally, nationally and internationally supply images to the newspapers they have a contract with. These pictures may be sent digitally to the newspaper's computer database so they can be viewed on-screen. The traditional method, however, is to send the images electronically to a special receiver/printer which produces hard print-outs. This process is called wiring.

An archive of pictures is kept by newspapers which contains pictures already published in the paper and a bank of head-and-shoulders portraits which are used daily to identify the key speakers in stories. Depending upon the size of the newspaper, this picture library may be staffed or it may be up to individual reporters and sub-editors to locate the required image in a filing cabinet.

Photographers will receive their briefing from the picture editor in person, by telephone or by radio. They may accompany the reporter to the job or go alone to a pre-arranged location and at a time set by the journalist. Not all images are commissioned by journalists, though. A good press photographer is always looking out for striking shots which tell a story of their own. Such pictures might depict a scorching hot summer's day or the first snows of winter, for example. Whatever the commission, press photographers go armed with a car-bootful of menacing looking machinery ranging from telescopic zoom lenses to capture the tiniest distant detail at a football match to wide-angle lenses to squeeze in the winning team for a group shot. They carry flash guns and tripods to cope with all conditions and terrains. One witty press photographer always carries a viking helmet in his kit and it's amazing how many pictures it turns up in!

Most press photographers favour 35 mm cameras because of their versatility and portability. These cameras are also appropriate for newspaper photojournalism as enlargements from 35 mm film also fit well onto newspaper pages because of their scale and dimensions. Medium or large-format cameras capture greater detail and are used for magazine covers or other images where high-quality definition is essential. Once on location, photographers load as much film into their camera as they are likely to need for that job and assess whether they need to use particular lenses, filters or other attachments. In addition to a technical analysis, photographers must employ their journalistic judgment in terms of what or who to include in the shot. They must visualize how the picture will look on the page and how well it supports the text, if any.

Last, but by no means least, if people are to be included in the image, the photographer must employ strong interpersonal communication skills to direct them into the right poses. Sensitivity is required as many people are wary of being photographed. A domineering attitude on the part of the photographer, or a subject left standing too long in the rain, can result in a disastrous picture. The photographer will snap several pictures from differing angles to be sure they have at least one good shot.

Even though the image has been captured by the camera, the photographer's job is far from over. Next comes a race against time to get the picture onto the page. If photographers have time, they will return to the newspaper office's own darkrooms, process the film and develop several photographs or ask the darkroom assistant to do it for them. Alternatively, if the picture is urgently needed but photographers must dash to another job, the film can be taken by courier to the newspaper office for processing.

Another method which has started to grow in popularity harnesses the latest in digital technology. Still-image video cameras, which are as portable as the basic 35 mm model, record images not on film but on the camera's internal memory or on a small floppy disk. Just like text produced on a computer, the camera can be attached to a telephone line and the pictures conveyed as a digital signal to a computer terminal on the picture editor's desk in a matter of seconds. Here they can be viewed as a complete image and can either be printed as a photograph or, if the newspaper is operating a full on-screen page make-up system, transmitted directly to the sub-editor's terminal.

If the film is to be processed in the darkroom, most newspapers have a machine into which the film is fed at one end and the processed negatives are dispatched at the other in a few minutes. This is far faster than the traditional hand method of processing and allows the photographer to get on with other jobs, such as preparing the developing chemicals. Either the photographer or the darkroom assistant will print a contact sheet which is done by laying the negatives on photographic paper to get thumbnail size versions of each shot. The best pictures can then be enlarged to produce two or three 10" × 8" photographs. A short, typed or computer-printed caption is attached and the pictures are handed to the newsdesk.

A newer method being used is to scan the negatives digitally on a machine resembling a photocopier. This converts the images into digital information which can be transmitted to a computer terminal and displayed on screen. Here the image can be adjusted using sophisticated software which allows time-consuming darkroom processes to be carried out in seconds. Using traditional methods, if a photograph was not bright enough, for example, it would have to be reprinted to alter the contrast. On computer, the brightness and contrast can be rectified at the touch of a keyboard button. Some newspapers are now storing their entire picture library in this way or on compact disk.

Once a photograph has been chosen, the editor may decide that only a portion of it is necessary or relevant. This process of excluding unwanted material in a picture is called cropping and is achieved swiftly on-screen because the sub-editor laying out the page can simply use a computer mouse to select the chosen part of a picture and enlarge or reduce it to the size required.

Press photography: job descriptions

Picture editor
Picture editors can come from a variety of backgrounds depending on the nature of the publication. Some are experienced press photographers who have worked their way up, winning awards along the way. Others come from an art and design background, particularly those working for broadsheets or supplements. They have a senior editorial role and, as well as overseeing the newspaper's entire photographic output, they attend daily news conferences presided over by the editor-in-chief and manage a budget. Their senior status requires management and interpersonal skills as well as visual creativity and expertise as a photographer.

Photographers

Newspaper photographers may be staff-based or self-employed, working on a freelance basis to cover individual jobs when requested or to work 8- or 12-hour shifts. There are several ways into photography. Some start out as darkroom assistants and work their way up, being trained on the job, while an increasing number take a pre-entry training course of some description, such as one validated by the National Council for the Training of Journalists or a related degree. They then apply for traineeships with newspapers. Others move from other areas of photography, such as weddings or corporate work.

On a personal level, newspaper photographers have to have strong personalities and a great deal of determination to get the image they want or their picture editor demands. They may have to talk their way through police cordons, persuade reluctant celebrities to pose or stake out a politician who has gone to ground.

Darkroom assistant

This is where many top photographers began their careers. This person is based mainly in the newspaper's darkroom and studio, supporting the photographers by developing pictures and maintaining the equipment. As they gain experience, darkroom assistants may even be given small photographic jobs of their own and are in an ideal situation to learn the craft. Some darkroom assistants have already done a basic course in photography or are trained on the job. They need to be well-organized and efficient because they are working with photographers operating under stressful and challenging conditions. There is more information about photography in Chapter 3 on magazines.

And now the editorial function comes to an end and the responsibility for the paper passes to production, but first the day's advertising must be incorporated.

Advertising

From this account of the working lives of journalists, it would appear that it is a painstaking craft to ensure objective, factual and detailed coverage. However, some would claim that advertisers have, potentially, a major stake in shaping the way local news is reported, especially if something bad is going to be written about them! Advertising can account for a high proportion of a newspaper's revenue, or even its entire income in the case of a free-distribution title, so most journalists are familiar with the story that leaves the ad manager gulping because it alienates and annoys a key customer. This may be the case in a small minority of tiny papers which are predominantly advertising sheets but any editor-in-chief worth his or her salt will vigorously defend editorial objectivity regardless of who is buying display or classified space. They will maintain that the reputation and survival of a newspaper lies in its responsible and unbiased reporting.

Advertising does play a crucial role in determining the look of the paper because it affects how much space is available for editorial. The advertising department sells space well in advance of the publication. The page-plans with markings indicating where the adverts will be featured are called 'shapes' and are passed to the editorial department to fill.

There are basically two main types of advertising, display and classified:

1. **Display advertising** This is obtained by dedicated newspaper sales representatives who not only sell space to shops and services but also advise their clients on developing their sales campaigns. Sales representatives are supported by the newspaper's art department who can translate the advertiser's ideas into attractive designs ready for printing. Display advertising is type- and graphics-based whereas classified advertising is type-based.
2. **Classified advertising** Most of this advertising is obtained by telephone and covers car, property and household equipment. Someone wishing to advertise an item will telephone the newspaper's Tele-ad department where the operator will key in the advert using a special computer package which can calculate the cost of the advertisement and will also sort the adverts into their appropriate classifications.

Once the last ads of the day have been sold editorial is advised how much space they have to fill. When all the editorial has been written and checked, the production process of the newspaper rolls into action.

Production

Within the last twenty years, newspaper production has undergone a technological revolution which has transformed not only the product but also the working lives of hundreds of thousands of people employed in the industry. The computerization of the industry has brought about historic repercussions, ranging from massive job cuts as once essential departments and personnel are wiped out, to the launch of hundreds of new weekly titles and a few regionals and nationals too.

Instead of grainy, greyish print, we now get our daily dose of news in gleaming technicolor and sparkling black-and-white with the added bonus in some cases that it stays on the page, not on our hands and clothes.

There is no doubt that with the threat of competition from broadcasting, the newspaper revolution has ensured that print news is more up-to-date, more visually attractive and more 'real'. The addition of colour, we are told, lends immediacy and drama to the still news image. The main impact of colour is that it has turned shop news-stands into a blaze of colour, ensuring papers remain attractive and competitive in the technological age.

Production journalists essentially work on the output of the newspaper. They are responsible for finding the best way of visually presenting information to the reader. The main type of production journalist is the sub-editor (sub) and this position will vary in rank and duty according to the nature of the title. Only a few years ago, in putting together a newspaper, sub-editors would have sat at a desk accompanied by stacks of paper, a cup of tea, a large pot of glue and pair of scissors. Today, in most newsrooms, the hot cup of tea will still be steaming by their side but the other objects will be replaced by one machine – the computer. The same fate has befallen the hot-metal Linotype machine, the typewriter and in some cases some human beings!

The subs desk

Larger newspapers have a subs desk divided into two tiers – top table and down-table, although the introduction of new technology and on-screen page make-up is blurring this distinction and on weeklies the job tends to be done by the same person. Top-table subs are responsible for designing page layouts, or shapes as they are often called. They are senior, experienced journalists who can assess the weight of a story and know best how to position it for the maximum impact. Down-table sub-editors deal more with the copy itself, taking instruction from the top-table subs. They must read through the copy and check it meticulously for accuracy, libel, spelling and grammar. Features may have to be cut to fit the available space as stipulated by the layout artist. Subs then go on to write headlines, captions and other devices which make the story readable and the page look interesting. A great deal of care and attention must be applied to ensuring that headlines tie in with the copy and do not mislead or alter the intention of the copy. The sub-editor's purpose is to make the page well-organized so that the reader gleans the information quickly and simply. Other sub-editing duties include selecting appropriate visual material to accompany text, selecting type formats, colours where applicable and seeing the page through to production.

Most of the work of production journalists, to varying degrees, is done using computers. At down-table level, copy is edited and measured and headlines and captions written to size using dedicated software. On many newspapers, the design of pages is still done on life-size dummy paper pages but the move is towards computers which allow subs to compose pages on templates on large computer screens. Pictures, adverts, text and headlines can be brought together on the one screen so the journalist is sure that all the different components will work together.

This is a simple description of how a page may be put together.

1. The advertising department sell display space on a page and send a page shape, with the advert clearly marked, to the subs desk. The sub has a set of stories from the newsdesk which, through discussion with the editor, have been allocated for inclusion on that page.
2. The sub is likely to know what will be the main focal point of the page, the lead, from the news conference and will mark out where it is to go, indicating the positioning of pictures, captions, headlines, by-lines (the name of the reporter) and any other typographical devices.
3. The process continues until the page is filled with the other stories, taking into account the overall 'look' of the paper which must be strictly adhered to. This means only certain typefaces and sizes of headline can be used or the

paper will lose its identity and look fragmented and incoherent.

4. At down-table level. The story will be checked for accuracy and readability, referring back to writers if there is any query, and edited down to size. Journalists, when writing their copy, are encouraged to put the least important information at the end of their story so that it will not be damaged if the sub has to slash off the last couple of paragraphs to fit the space. Headlines and other details have to be written carefully and must fit the available slot exactly. A letter over allocated length and stories may overlap.

5. Once stories are subbed to the desired length and design they are assigned to the relevant page queue. Here they are merged with other stories intended for that page to create one file and the information is sent to the typesetter machine which outputs a dummy copy (proof) for inspection.

6. A journalist views the proof, approves it and assigns the file to a queue from where it will be typeset onto bromide paper, which provides a good surface from which the page can be reproduced.

7. The bromide copy is physically pasted onto a grid sheet along with pictures and advertisements.

8. The pasted-up page is scanned to turn the information into a digital message. If it is for a national newspaper printed off-site, the information may be transmitted digitally to these satellite plants which are often located in the north of England or Scotland so that areas furthest from London still get their papers on time containing the latest stories. For example, News International has a satellite printing press at Knowsley, near Liverpool. At these plants, the data is output as a negative onto recorders loaded with film cassettes containing laser sensitive film which is used to create a printing plate. Transmission of all that information takes around four minutes with a further one minute to develop and process the full page negative. New transmission methods are being pioneered which could speed up this process further so that page plates can be converted into data and printed digitally, instead of having to produce new printing plates at the satellite stations. If the paper is printed in-house, the process is simpler with a negative being taken of the page bromide which is then used to create the plate.

Printing

The web-offset litho process has all but replaced traditional hot metal printing methods. Unlike in older processes where printing was largely a manual, dirty process, nowadays most preparation for printing is done with computer technology. This dramatic technological innovation which peaked in the mid 1980s caused a national wave of opposition with its accompanying massive job cuts. Whole production departments were wiped out overnight creating bitter resentment. Many say that was just the start.

Web offset works on the principle that ink, being oil-based, does not mix with water. Printing plates are therefore designed so that white or blank areas are receptive to water while any areas that need to be printed are receptive to ink. By this method, the paper can be printed on both sides simultaneously. Where colour is used, as it is with most national, regional and local tabloid newspapers these days, the process is rather more complicated but works to the same principle. Any colour to be printed must first be separated into its four main components which are cyan (blue), magenta (red) and yellow and black. The colours are laid down on the page in the order cyan, black, magenta, yellow, the black being used to give the image definition. If you look at the colour bars on the side of a colour newspaper page, you will see the breakdown and intensity of the colours used. Colour seps, as they are called – short for separations – are prepared using computer scanners which produce four separate negatives. The negatives are exposed onto ultra-violet light sensitive aluminium printing plates using a vacuum to ensure good contact. This causes a chemical reaction which makes certain areas attract ink and reject water. A special bar code – a pre-ink curve – is placed on the plate which sets basic ink values onto the press cylinder. This virtually eliminates wastage and assures the paper is printed to a high quality soon after the presses start to roll. The plates are processed and developed in a plate processor which has three tanks: a development tank, wash tank and a fixer tank which stops the plate from oxidizing. The aluminium plate is bent in a plate bender and fixed to the press, sprayed with water and the printing starts. In the case of colour, once the seps have been made, several colour proofs are made for each colour set to ensure perfect reproduction.

Prior to printing, the appropriate number of printing units are selected according to the paper's pagination and number of colours, and appropriate printing information is punched into the press computer, such as paper, fold, ink and tension. Each press has a dummy run to check they are functioning correctly. Finally, the plates are locked onto the plate cylinders. Within minutes, the first saleable copies run off the presses. For the rest of the printing process, the system and the outcoming papers are monitored very carefully.

Some presses, such as those recently installed at the News International plant at Wapping, are capable of running off 80 000 copies per hour. The paper, known as newsprint, is fed to the presses robotically and the whole printing process is computer controlled and calibrated.

Once printed, papers are compiled, folded, baled and delivered onto delivery vans destined for shops or depots all by machinery.

Even in these high-tec days, seeing the presses roll can be a very exciting experience, particularly if it is your story on the front page! The sheer speed involved in production today can mean that from the first telephone call to the newsdesk, to the story reaching the street, can take an hour! Who says print isn't as immediate as radio or TV.

Distribution

Regional and local newspapers will be taken directly by their own or contract delivery companies to retail outlets. Local weekly freesheets will be centrally stored then collected by deliverers who post them through front doors throughout the area.

At the other end of the scale, the distribution of national newspapers is a meticulously choreographed process spanning thousands of miles each day and night. Papers are transported by train but most commonly by freight lorries to wholesalers who service around 46 000 newsagents and selling points nationwide. A proportion are sent to airports for delivery to Northern Ireland, the Republic of Ireland, the Channel Islands, Europe and overseas.

The newsagent then organizes the supplies which are sold from their shop or dispatched by the estimated 300 000 newspaper boys and girls in Britain. Unsold copies are stored by the newsagent until the weekend when they are taken away by the wholesaler. Most of these leftover newspapers are sold for recycling into newsprint which will be used to produce new newspapers.

NEW AND FUTURE DEVELOPMENTS IN NEWSPAPER JOURNALISM

While the basic appeal of newspapers has changed very little over the past twenty years, modern technology has transformed the industry to bring readers a faster service. Old-fashioned typewriters have long-since been abandoned and newspapers have joined the computer age. Journalists are now using electronic keyboards to input their stories and features directly to the typesetting system. Direct input not only saves on time and staff costs, it means up-to-the-minute coverage of all news, sport and TV programmes for the reader.

It does not matter whether reporters work in the office or not. Journalists are given laptop computers – Tandy, IBM, Apple etc. – which they can plug into a telephone socket or hook up to a receiver to send their words as a series of beeps and squeaks to the waiting mother computer. Pictures can be sent by computer directly from the scene of the event to the photo desk in just the same way. Any hard copy, that which is written on paper by freelances for instance, is immediately typed in so it can be read on screen by the newsdesk.

These networks are enormous. They have to cope with hundreds of people using various VDU workstations, they must store millions of megabytes-worth of information both in terms of copy, advertisements, pictures and software, and they have to work fast. Newsroom computers are the first to feel the force of the journalist's rolled-up notebook at the first sign of a processing delay.

News agencies and other organizations now have the equipment to enable them to file information directly onto newspaper computer screens. Up-to-the minute share-prices from the Stock Exchange and unit trust prices from Extel are beamed onto City desk screens as if by magic.

New printing technology has enabled papers cheaply to harness the public appeal of colour. Just about every national newspaper and many regionals are stuffed with colour magazines, partly to boost sales and also to appeal to advertisers who were being lured away by the attraction of the moving television image. Since the mid-1980s, a host of new print titles have come into existence mainly due to the innovations in new technology. While the cost of the machinery needed is sky high, it is less labour-intensive than old methods and several titles can easily be launched from the one office.

Over the decades there has been much speculation about the future of newspapers and magazines. Broadcast news, offering instant sounds and eyewitness pictures at the push of a button, at one time appeared to threaten the print industry. It was speculated that a consumer culture used to high-tech innovations would want news-to-go. We would no longer want to sit down and read pages and pages of grey type. So far, this has not been the case. In fact the advent of new technology has made the whole process of producing newspapers so much cheaper, faster and easier that a wealth of new titles has sprung up, particularly in the local and regional sector where there is still great demand among readers and advertisers for community-based news stories.

Introduced into this country in the early 1980s, desktop publishing (DTP) has been one of the most important recent technological developments and has been gaining rapid momentum within the print industry ever since because by allowing the user to do what was once the jobs of several people, it has slashed the production costs of publishing newspapers and magazines. Less cynically, it has improved the work of journalists. By cutting out the need for laborious typing on paper and allowing editing and typesetting to be done on one machine, DTP has cut production time drastically, giving journalists more time to write. At one time, type had literally to be cast in hot metal and pages were physically constructed on a platform which was known as the stone. DTP has wiped out the need for traditional typesetting by enabling pages to be spewed out as a photographic negative which can be transformed into a printing plate in a fraction of the time. Consisting primarily of a powerful personal computer and printer, it allows the user to carry out all the major publishing functions – writing, editing, design and graphics – on one machine and print out the end result which may be a house magazine, brochure, newsletter and so on.

Because in DTP, one person can potentially do the job of several, the cost of production has been cut drastically. Preparing for the printing process can be done faster and more cheaply without any loss in quality. Most publishers use DTP in one form or another. Those that don't are replacing old equipment with DTP systems so that pages can be made up on screen and design, typesetting and other previously expensive processes can be done in-house. On newspapers and journals, many of the jobs that were once done in the print room are now done by journalists. Proofreading can be done on screen, for example. The former wire rooms of daily papers, many of which would house half-a-dozen teleprinters, have now largely been replaced by computerized receiving systems so the stories reach the monitors on the news-desk. It is certainly a skill the aspiring journalist cannot ignore, whatever medium they have ambitions to enter, as computers are used in radio and television to an increasing degree.

And, while technology is clearly culling many traditional jobs in print, the cheap cost of production means there are more opportunities cropping up for computer-minded candidates.

In America newspapers are putting pages onto computer networks and offering facsimile services so that recipients, especially in the business world, can see stories on screen the moment they break or get vital information over the fax machine well before the paper is printed. Time will tell whether the market demand will justify the large expense of installing the appropriate equipment.

One of the lasting attractions of newspapers when compared with radio and television is that the contents can be read anywhere at any time because they are so portable. Pioneers in the USA are coming up with A4 electronic computer tablets which are light, cheap, easy on batteries and can access information without mains or telephone cables. Perhaps in the long-run, instead of taking the tabloids, we'll be taking the tablets.

As well as competition from broadcast media, other factors also threaten the future of newspapers, mainly by luring advertisers to lucrative markets like home shopping. One answer to this in America is the concept of the interactive newspaper. According to the Newspaper Society, local newspapers in the US are making around £100 000 extra revenue a year from 0890-style telephone voice-dating agencies which allow would-be boyfriends and girlfriends to hear what each other sound like as well as reading descriptions about them in the paper. This is just the tip of the iceberg as the same service could be applied to advertising and information services such as sport and weather.

Not everyone is convinced, however, with the argument that we will all end up calling up news on a computer screen. But the media correspondent of *The Guardian* is among those who feels computers have changed journalists' lives for the better: 'I doubt many journalists would go back to the old way of doing things. We have more power over our copy and can monitor its progress even once it has gone into production.' A reporter using a portable computer can access library information, agency copy and send messages to other staff on screen. They can use it at home and gain access to all the same information there, enabling them to work late at night or on a Sunday without having to come into the office.

The editor of the *Liverpool Echo* agrees and believes that there will follow a re-evaluation of traditional roles in print production: 'Whether, for example, it's necessary for journalists and sub-editors to be two separate things, whether it's possible for photographers to write stories and writers to take pictures.' Camera technology has made some cameras much easier to use and computers with built-in spelling and grammar checks can help the photographer who once had concerns about writing stories feel more confident. The editor continues:

> At its best it is a very important specialism on both sides. At its most mundane it's hard to believe that a business reporter interviewing a managing director can't take a picture of him sat behind his desk or that the photographer who takes a fantastic picture of a child playing rounders in a school can't come back and write a very appropriate story to go with it. I'm not saying the two roles will merge but overlap will come.

Many publications appointing trainees automatically equip their recruits with a variety of skills because it is felt that it makes them better reporters and writers to have spent some time processing other people's material in the sub-editor's department.

However these recruits may eventually find themselves having to be skilled not only in writing for their paper but also for television, all within the same office. It looks increasingly as though cable TV will offer a partnership opportunity for regional newspapers by giving them a new way of delivering their news through local cable stations. The idea is increasingly tempting for regional newspapers when they look across to America and see a link between city newspapers and city news stations. Cable companies which have bought up most contracts for cabling cities in the UK are looking to provide a news service. The one place in town where a news service is already up and running and is paid for is the newspaper and a lot of newspapers will be looking to see whether there is a mutually beneficial deal to be struck. There could develop a situation where newspapers are distributed via print for those who want it in that form and via cable for those who want it on screen in the form of a programme. Supporters of this idea argue that sales of the newspapers will not be jeopardized because any half-hour television news programme will only give a fraction of the information contained in the newspaper. In fact, such a partnership could protect the traditional paper's newsgathering and keep it manned to the sort of levels and quality that we've had traditionally.

In conclusion, the print revolution may so far have transformed the working lives of journalists and the way newspapers reach the newsstands. As we look to the future and the likely developments in digital imaging and text production, we must consider whether this might not also revolutionize the content of our news and open the way for more widespread fabrication or manipulation of information, particularly as competition for audience with broadcast media looks set to become more heated.

3

Magazines

The distinctions between what constitutes a newspaper and a magazine are often very blurred. Some periodicals may have the physical appearance of a newspaper but only be published quarterly with largely feature-based content. Conversely, publications may come out weekly with a high, up-to-the minute news content yet may still be deemed a magazine because of their slightly glossier format. You would think that with approximately 7700 titles on the market at the latest count, magazines would be far and away the largest mass medium. In fact, they come third in line after television and newspapers in terms of audience/reader figures, but they have a unique rapport with their readership and their appeal is strong and enduring for readers, advertisers and their publishers and staff. The periodical industry is also one area of the media that is experiencing rapid growth. Figures published by the Periodical Publishers Association say the number of titles has increased by a staggering 74% over the last 12 years. This is very exciting news for the prospective journalist as many new opportunities are opening up in this diverse, flourishing sector.

As you will see, while many titles have vast readerships, they are not circulated via newsagents which means there is a large assortment of periodicals which potential employees may not know about. Later in this section, there will be more on how you can find out about these magazines.

Some magazines, especially glossy and art-and-design titles, have to be prepared months before they reach the newsagents because they involve highly intricate production techniques. By virtue of magazines' extended shelf-life, editors have to envisage what is going to interest their readers in three months' time, not just today. So journalistic values about content and approach will be different on a monthly title than they will be on a weekly.

For many of us, buying a magazine is like giving ourselves a treat. Magazines usually cost more, for a start; they may be made of thicker, glossier paper, and they may be full of lush images to gaze upon. Magazine producers, especially in the leisure market, take into account the tactile pleasures of possessing a magazine as well as the informative nature of the content and publishers invest a great deal in production technology to achieve the best finish to suit readers and advertisers alike.

One of the most significant transformations in magazine publishing came about due to new technology which has enabled hosts of magazines to be published cheaply with good colour reproduction all in the one 'house'. Magazines, perhaps more than other media, have harnessed the latest innovations in technology to the extent that some titles are beginning to appear in CD-Rom format, that is on disk to be read from a computer screen as an alternative to paper. This is probably the tip of an electronic iceberg as is discussed in later chapters. The main benefit of new technology to publishers has been the low cost of publishing several titles from the one building. Costs are reduced and production times decreased because computers can perform many more tasks which were once laborious and expensive.

Added to that is the response from software manufacturers who have created programmes enabling all aspects of a magazine's production – from writing to layout to pictures to typesetting – to be carried out on the one machine. What this means for the journalist is that they will have to be confident with using a keyboard at the very least. Preferably, applicants should be able to demonstrate some element of multi-skilling, this means that they can participate in many aspects of production and can talk in the language used by photographers, typographers, designers and printers as well as that of writers.

THE SHAPE OF THE MAGAZINE INDUSTRY

The magazine industry is sometimes described as a cottage industry. It seems bizarre, considering it is one of the most highly sophisticated and innovative parts of the media industry, to endow it with rural or rustic connotations. What is meant is that large publishers provide the roof over a series of smaller individual dedicated units which are the specific titles within their group. They have small staffs but bring in a great deal of advertising and revenue. It looks as if the market for magazines will continue to grow, creating more and more job opportunities, as society demands more leisure-time interests. Magazines fall mainly into two categories: consumer titles, which provide entertainment and leisure-time information, and business and professional publications covering issues relevant to people's working lives.

Consumer magazines

These are the titles we are most familiar with as they adorn the racks in newsagents' shops, supermarkets and other outlets in their hundreds. The most visible are women's titles of which new ones are cropping up all the time. There are currently around 100 women's titles with a combined circulation of more than 400 million. Other consumer titles are targeted towards an audience with a specific interest such as sport, arts, hobbies and music. While the majority of consumer titles are published monthly, weeklies do better in the marketplace and represent three out of every four consumer magazines sold. The cover prices for these titles can vary enormously as can the number of pages and overall print and paper quality. Many titles are also purchased by annual subscription directly from the publishers by loyal readers.

This category of periodical is further subdivided into **general interest** and **specialist**. General interest magazines have wide appeal to a large audience. Women's magazines such as *Marie Claire*, television listings titles such as *Radio Times* and home-related monthlies such as *House and Garden* fall into this sector. Magazines catering for a hobby, interest or issue such as BBC *Gardener's World*, *What Car* and *New Scientist* fall into the specialist category.

There are also hybrids. These exist particularly in the computer market where some titles contain items of an in-depth technical nature which can also be understood by the wider audience. *MacUser* is such a title.

Most of the major magazine titles are owned by relatively few large publishing companies. In the consumer sector, representing general and specialist interest publications, IPC Magazines is the largest publisher. Among its most popular titles are *TV Times*,

Woman's Weekly, Woman, Ideal Home and *Shoot!*. Aggregate weekly sales total 3.5 million for its weekly women's titles alone. Other consumer title publishers include National Magazine Company (*Cosmopolitan, House Beautiful*), Conde Nast (*Vogue*), BBC Magazines, EMAP and Readers Digest.

Consumer magazines derive just under two-thirds of their revenue from the cover price of each title, the remainder coming from advertising. By contrast, the other main sector of periodicals, business and professional magazines, obtain on average just under 80% of their revenue from advertising and the rest from sales. Advertisers are willing to pay more to be in these magazines because they go directly to the market the advertiser wishes to reach.

Business and professional magazines

Business and professional periodicals represent one of the biggest growth areas in journalism and reach millions of specialist markets weekly and monthly. This is a larger sector than consumer publishing with some 4000 titles.

These magazines are aimed directly at people working within a specific business area. Titles including *The Grocer, The Architects' Journal* and *Hospital Doctor* demonstrate just how diverse the range of publications within this genre is. Each magazine provides the reader with an update of the latest news affecting their industry as well as publishing relevant features. They can also act as a noticeboard, publicizing events and conferences and a format for readers to air their views via the letters page.

In addition to providing a service to their readership, business magazines act as a major source of news for national newspapers, often being the first medium to report on a new product launch or business merger. They have the scope to delve into issues in much more detail than general-interest magazines or newspapers which can give a great deal of satisfaction to the journalist wanting to dig beneath the surface.

Publications aimed at the professions largely sprang up around the time of the Great Exhibition of the 1850s. Victorians were promoting self-improvement and several titles were launched as the professions started to be more clearly defined, such as *The Builder* and *The Engineer*. Following on from the success of these all-encompassing titles, more specific publications dealing with sectional interests were introduced until, in the last 20 to 30 years, publishers have found niche market populations upon which to launch a whole host of periodicals. Today, we have a massive proliferation of titles with strictly controlled circulations aimed exactly at key personnel.

These publications offer real opportunities for in-depth reporting on complex issues and sometimes give recruits excellent allround experience of periodical production at all levels. Many go on to work for the national newspapers but a large proportion choose to stay within this sector because they find it more rewarding. For graduates with specialist skills, working on one of these titles can be a rewarding way of using knowledge gained during their degree study. Some writers are required to possess a high degree of technical knowledge and expertise in their area. Coupled with experience on a general newspaper, this can lead to a specialist post on a national newspaper.

Among the bigger business and professional publishing companies are EMAP Business Publishing, Reed Business Publishing Group, Morgan-Grampian, Haymarket Magazines and VNU Business Publications. But there are many other small, independently published titles catering for specialized markets.

This niche marketing is directly responsible for the dramatic growth in periodicals being published. Magazines are renowned for their intensive research of potential new areas to cover and this has been reflected in the launch of titles for distribution to tightly defined markets.

Controlled circulation magazines are aimed directly at their readership and are largely distributed free to people who can benefit from them. A great deal of market research goes into building up a profile of the readership and addressing them directly through editorial and advertising.

Controlled circulation is a practice imported from the USA where databases storing the identities of key-players within specified businesses are accessed to give publishers a strictly defined market for their product. It is a common means of distribution in this sector. They can attract more advertising on the basis that, for example, they purport to reach, say 95% of the top personnel within that market. Consequently, some periodicals will reject new readers and keep their circulation limited rather than dilute the penetration of their product. One senior figure in the magazine industry says: 'The product is not the magazines but the readers – the reader is of paramount importance. Without them you'll fail so a great deal of research and thought goes into developing that relationship.'

Some business-to-business publications, such as *Construction News*, published weekly by Thomson, do not use controlled circulation but are subscription-based. The editor-in-chief explains that the cover price is an incentive to readership – 'People will tend to read what they have paid for ' – and indicates the quality of the publication. The cover price also brings in significant revenue for a weekly with an above-average number of editorial staff, currently 20.

Other types of magazines

In-house magazines are read by customers of a big retail store or employees of a large multinational corporation. For example, British Nuclear Fuels has a weekly title for its workforce, *BNFL News*, which aims to keep employees based at its many sites in touch with new developments and with one another. Customer publications are another expanding area. These are produced by or for retail outlets or service providers for their customers and contain editorial and information about products and services. These are sometimes produced by agencies for the organization, for example, in the case of Sainsbury's magazine.

Academic journals, often owned by societies as well as publishers, are the first outlet for much of the latest medical, arts and scientific research. These journals do not have the same editorial structure or job opportunities as other magazines. They tend to be run by an editorial board and are the outlet or showcase for work of a highly technical or academic nature.

What is the difference between writing for a magazine and a newspaper?

According to the editorial training and development manager for IPC magazines, being a journalist on a magazine is not inherently different from working as a journalist in any other medium. 'A journalist is a journalist,' she says. 'You need a critical, enquiring mind and you are bringing information and excitement to the reader'.

When writing for a newspaper, radio or television report, journalists have a notion of their audience which will tend to be broad and essentially an attempt to grab the attention of the largest number of people. Working for a magazine is different in that journalists will have a clearer picture in their mind of the targeted reader, in terms of categories which may include age, career status, possibly gender, hobby interests and so on. By their very nature, magazines must harness a deep rapport with their readership.

In the consumer bracket, particularly teenagers', women's, and increasingly men's, lifestyle market, feature writers have to put a great deal of themselves into their work. Articles about relationships and emotions often require journalists to write candidly and openly which can be very demanding. The language used in such magazines will tend to be carefully worded to harness an intimate, warm conversational tone. They try, in essence, to be like a friend or confidant to the reader.

Whereas news journalism tends to require objectivity on the pat of the writer, many consumer periodicals thrive to a great extent on comment and opinion. The music press is one example of periodicals containing criticism, which may offer a refreshing challenge to potential journalists. A further key characteristic of magazine journalists is their ability to write. While in newspapers and other hard news media, words are used simply and concisely, magazine articles are often longer and more detailed and have to paint an intricate picture for the reader. This means magazines can be a rewarding career opportunity for the journalist who wants to use language and vocabulary more creatively.

Before we examine the roles of those working in magazine journalism, here is an example of a story and how it might be covered.

The celebrity interview

1. The Editor-in-Chief holds his monthly planning meeting to discuss ideas for the February issue. It is only a month away from production and already many of the pages, including fashion and a few features, are complete. The Editor-in-Chief is considering ideas for the main story of the month which can

be used as a major attraction for selling the publication. January, when the magazine will hit the newstands, is a dull month as Christmas is over, so readers are looking for something dynamic and colourful to make the issue stand out from its competition. One of the section editors, who has good contacts in the music industry, has received a tip-off that an enigmatic pop star who rarely gives interviews is coming to town to finish producing his album. With a good head start, she might be able to spend some time at the studios and try to get an interview. This would not only make a good feature but a glamorous front page photograph.

2. The section editor, who has been assigned to write the feature, spends a day on the telephone trying to reach the star's press officer in America but, because of the time difference, has to continue making calls from home. Two days later, the press officer returns her call and says the star will not be giving any interviews. Not deterred, she contacts the recording studio to find out what other artists will be recording there at the same time as the star and decides to use her time usefully by interviewing up-and-coming performers while trying to get an audience with the star. She knows from experience that a foot-in-the-door pushy approach does not always work. Subtlety and developing trust with contacts takes time but can sometimes pay off in the end. She has been given two weeks to complete the feature which gives her time to spend a few hours a day at the studio and the rest of her time doing other background research on the artiste and completing the mountain of other stories she has on her list.

3. The journalist has spent three days at the studios and has carried out many successful interviews with rising stars which she knows will make interesting reading, especially as one might become a huge star in their own right. She has spoken to many of the star's entourage, shared a joke with them and has even interviewed one or two about their experiences. Despite pleading, she has not managed to speak to the star himself and it's not looking hopeful as security is tight. The deadline is looming and she needs to think how she is going to angle her piece to make it interesting even though she hasn't caught a glimpse of the star. After

consulting the Editor-in-Chief, it is decided a feature about her relentless pursuit of the star, including interviews with his closest confidantes, might be the best original, tongue-in-cheek approach. She begins:

We seek him here, we seek him there, we seek him every-where. Week after week we are bombarded with startling photographs and stunning record reviews yet when we tried to make a date with him as he fine-tuned his latest release, this massive star turned into the invisible man ...

4. A front page picture is needed so she speaks to the Art Editor who looks through the magazine's own picture library and contacts an agency. Because many pictures of the star have been used elsewhere, she is committed to getting an original shot for the front cover. Approaches to the star's press officer are fruitless. 'He's too busy recording to find time for a photoshoot' is the reply. The Art Editor commissions a free-lance photographer to wait outside the studio to try to catch a shot of the star arriving or leaving. The photographer sits in his car for two days until he realizes he has been spotted and the star is sneaking out through another exit.

5. Meanwhile, with only five days to go before the copy dead-line, the journalist asks the editorial assistant to find press cut-tings about the star and prepare a back catalogue of his sin-gles, albums and videos for publication while she devotes her energies to getting as much information as possible from his crew for her feature. The editorial assistant starts by sifting through the magazine's own archive of journalistic material which is filed under the name of the artiste. Several national newspapers and magazines also run a library service on the Internet computer network which allows subscribers access to an enormous amount of information if their computer is linked to a telephone line. The editorial assistant does not rely on the information from other publications so she checks details with the star's fan club. The Editor-in-Chief is disap-pointed. The front-page photograph has not materialized so, as the production deadline creeps closer, he decides he will have to print a feature and use a front cover which have been kept on stand-by for this eventuality.

6. The day before her deadline, the journalist works well into the night writing her feature as colourfully as she can in the hope it might be included somewhere in the magazine. She needs to check one fact so she decides to go to the studio on her way home. On her way out she stops for a snack in the restaurant next door. Much to her surprise, she sees many of the star's band. As she is now a familiar and trusted face, they call her over to join them. Much to her surprise, the man she has been pursuing for the past week and a half is seated right next to her. After gentle persuasion, he agrees to a very short interview which she records on her cassette recorder as they eat. His press officer agrees to send the magazine exclusive publicity pictures in advance just in time for the front cover.

7. The exhilarated journalist goes straight back to the office and retrieves her feature on her VDU. Luckily, her feature is almost complete and contains all the details she requires. She decides to stick to her original approach of cataloguing her efforts to track down the star but builds up 'will she or won't she' tension to keep the reader in suspense and wanting to read more. She inserts the actual interview at the end of the feature. The entire piece is written in a style that is appropriate to a young and informed audience. She introduces her interviewee in the following way which helps to contrast ironically the immense fame of the star with the mundanity of the surroundings, as if such a chance meeting could happen to any of the readers.

'Coffee, black, no sugar.' It's a plain request but when he says it with his mid-Atlantic husky drawl you are reminded of the way he whispers provocatively through his more explicit tracks. He says 'coffee' but he might as well be suggesting something a whole lot more fun. Can he summon the emotion to sing about love at 3am on a rainy night in Birmingham? 'Yeah, sure ...'

The interview proceeds as a set of questions and answers complete with 'erms', sighs and other natural forms of punctuation to describe to the entranced reader every characteristic of their hero's behaviour.

8. The next day, it is clear the magazine art department will have to rush to produce a layout for the feature which covers

four pages as it is such a major achievement for the publication. Two other items will be removed for publication in a later
issue. The production department is informed of the alteration
because printing plates will have to be altered to ensure the
magazine is printed in the right order.

9. The Art Editor puts the publicity shots in an electronic scan-
ner so they can be viewed on his VDU. He uses a computer
software package that allows him to manipulate the image so
any flaws are airbrushed away. He composes the magazine's
front page by importing the masthead and other text which
will overlay the image. The Editor-in-Chief approves the cover
as it appears on screen.

10. The Editor-in-Chief examines the copy and suggests any styl-
istic or other amendments. Suggestions will be made for the
insertion of additional information if required. Sub-editors will
use the available material to draw up a page plan and display
the story appropriately. Feature pages will be subbed first and
news pages closer to the production deadline so that the information contained is most up-to-date and to allow for last-minute
alterations. Depending on the type of computer technology
employed by the publication – and the majority are highly
sophisticated – the pages may be composed as a visual image
on screen, where text, images and headlines are displayed together as a replica of the page to be printed. Or it may be done
on paper. This means text and images are printed out separately
then pasted onto a grid. Once the page proofs are available, that
is when a dummy print-out has been output by the printer, it will
be closely scrutinized or proofread by the Editor-in-Chief for
style and accuracy. Once the pages have been approved they
will be downloaded to a typesetter which converts the page
onto photographic film in preparation for printing (see the section on the production process of newspapers in Chapter 2).

What this example should demonstrate is that, while magazines
have to be carefully planned in advance both in terms of content
and production, human frailties and unexpected events can still
crop up. It just goes to show that no matter how advanced the

technology is that is used to produce the magazine, journalism is very much an activity led by human emotions and actions. That is what makes it such an unpredictable and exciting profession.

THE STRUCTURE OF A MAGAZINE'S EDITORIAL DEPARTMENT

Flick through the pages of most magazines and you will see tucked away in a corner a list of the publication's staff. The thing that will probably strike you is just how few people work in editorial and how many work in the other departments. It is certainly true that magazines tend to have fewer editorial staff than newspapers because they commission many of the articles and features from freelance writers. But the advertising, sales and promotional staff you will see listed may not work solely for that title either. As you have read, many periodicals are produced by one publishing house and some staff may be responsible for more than one title within the group. The figure below gives one possible breakdown of how a magazine's staff may be organized. But as magazines vary so much, many other permutations exist. The remainder of this chapter will be devoted to examining the roles of those who work in editorial and how a magazine is produced. If you would like to learn more about advertising and printing processes, refer to the relevant sections in Chapter 2 (Newspapers).

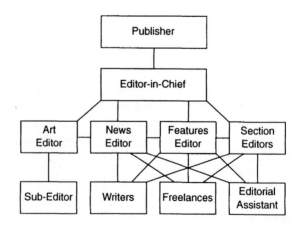

Magazines use the services of thousands of journalists both full-time and on a freelance basis. There are around 250 magazine publishing companies centred mainly around London and the Home Counties. These range in size from half-a-dozen to 2000 staff. There are approximately 20 000 people employed in magazines in this country of which about a quarter are writers and editors. A small number of major companies, for example, Reed, EMAP and Thomson, account for most of these employees.

The core staff are usually a great deal smaller than on a national daily newspaper. Depending on whether it is a weekly or monthly title, there may be as few as half a dozen full-time staff on a magazine and their roles may not be purely defined. For instance, in any one week, a magazine writer may also sub-edit pages and stand in for the editor-in-chief at an official function.

Both consumer and business magazines keep every door open when it comes to looking for recruits. Typical candidates will follow the traditional journalism entry routes – degree, then a postgraduate course in newspaper or periodical journalism then a traineeship on a title. But these are only one part of what is needed to service properly such diverse markets and interests. Many journalists come into magazines through non-traditional routes, for example a career in nursing, and it is these individuals, offering a specialist or technical knowledge who are actively sought out.

As a scientist or engineer, you may not be the first to discover something new about the structure of the atom, but you might be the first to deliver that news to the world, to speak to the experts and carry the great responsibility of making the information understandable and accessible to the public.

Once in, career prospects for multiskilled magazine journalists are good whether you want to stay on one title or move around. The sheer amount of 'movement' within the sector means promotion can be fast.

There is no easy way of writing generally about jobs in magazines because descriptions and roles differ between titles as much as do the subjects written about. The number of staff and their roles on a title will vary according to whether the magazine is published weekly or monthly and some generalizations can be made.

Some monthlies, particularly in the business sector, may only have two full-time journalists to oversee production of the title. They will commission features from freelance contributors and will enlist the part-time services of a designer to lay out the pages. A weekly title, particularly in the consumer sector, will inevitably have more staff. As well as the editor-in-chief there may be section heads, chief subs, feature writers, news reporters and designers.

Much depends on the nature of what is being written. There is clearly no point in employing journalists full-time who can only write about a specific area. They will be called upon on a free-lance basis to contribute copy as and when needed.

Staff complements tend to consist of a mixture of general and, on the specialist periodicals, technically qualified journalists. The hierarchy of skills and roles existing on newspapers does not occur in many magazines. There is usually a blurring of distinctions between different jobs.

Magazine journalism: job descriptions

Here is a rough guide to the different roles which may appear on a publication:

Publisher/publishing director

This person is responsible for the overall management of editorial, advertising, production, distribution, in fact all areas of the publication process. They have to exercise both sound business judgment and also be able to manage a large team of staff and a budget. This person may have several titles to oversee. Inevitably it is someone who has considerable knowledge of every process and who will usually have worked for a number of years in editorial and maybe also in sales.

Editor-in-chief/assistant editor/departmental editor

These people have the role of overseeing and managing the editorial production of the magazine from generating story ideas right through to ensuring the printed pages are of the highest quality. They may have overall responsibility or be in charge of one specific aspect. On a women's magazine, for instance, you might have a fashion editor, features editor, news and style editor and others. The editor-in-chief is at the helm but may be so busy with managerial and budgetary duties that most of the journalistic tasks are delegated to their deputies. The editor-in-chief has overall responsibility for the commercial success of the title. They will know their market intimately and understand its needs and how the publication should respond to them. On a day-to-day level, they will be responsible for managing both the advertising and editorial departments, recruiting staff and allocating resources. They will often stamp their personality on the publication by, for example, writing a leader, which is the introduction for each issue to set the tone of the publication and maintain a close, friendly relationship with their readership. This is especially so in consumer titles where the editor will talk as if having a one-to-one conversation with the readers about their lives.

In magazines, assistant editor/departmental editor is often the title given to a reporter or feature writer as it encompasses their other duties including commissioning copy from outside sources, such as freelance writers or agencies, plus sub-editing and layout.

As a team, the editor-in-chief and deputies will do the following.

1. Plan future issues, often months ahead, at weekly meetings. They will discuss ideas for features and campaigns together and with other magazine personnel including picture editors, designers and advertising executives so everyone is aware of proposals for that issue and the role they will be playing in its production.
2. They must ensure copy is commissioned from staff writers or from their network of freelance contributors. Editors will frequently produce a written brief for writers which is a sheet of paper bearing the title of the feature, date of publication, deadline and details of the subject matter and approach they wish the journalist to adopt. If it is to be written by a freelance contributor, the brief will also show the fee for the work.
3. If it is a magazine with a small staff, editors may also personally write features and articles.

These roles require considerable experience and sound judgment. They have to know their readership intimately to ensure that copy is pitched at the right level and that editorial content is accessible and familiar. They also have to know how to liaise with staff and get the best work from them which demands patience and encouragement as well as tact.

Art editor/designer

While the person is not a journalist, their role in devising the visual identity of a publication is both a highly creative and responsible job. The feel or look of a magazine will play a major role, certainly as much as the subject matter, in determining whether it will be bought or read. The wrong colour or typeface could be off-putting to the target audience or create completely the wrong impression. On the other hand, magazines often adopt a free and liberal approach to design and will not shy away from experimenting with and innovating new typefaces and layout styles. Art editors and designers have a strong background in art and design and know the technical side of periodical production inside out so they can produce the right materials. They have an innate sense of knowing what is eye-catching without being off-putting. Their role is to showcase and complement the text, not detract from it, as good layouts enhance and contribute to the meaning of the text and images. In the 1980s, corresponding with the launch of style magazines, designers began to take a leading role in directing the 'feel' of publications and became senior members of staff sometimes with a place on the board of directors. Depending on the size of the publication, a designer may be employed on a freelance basis to conceive the magazine's identity and format before a relaunch. Alternatively, they may be a staff member with daily duties which may include the following:

1. Conceiving a format for the publication and a visual identity. This involves determining appropriate typefaces, use and positioning of images, type of paper and many other factors to ensure the magazine appeals to and stimulates its audience.
2. Briefing and overseeing the work of the magazine's sub-editors who are responsible for making all of the different elements fit on to the page to the required style.
3. Liaising with editorial team and responding with visual solutions to proposed themes, for example, suggesting ideas for the appearance of a fashion shoot.
4. On some magazines, layouts will often be prepared ahead of the submission of photographs or text and designers will inform appropriate departments as to how many words or images they should commission.
5. Following the production of the magazine through to printing and overseeing aspects such as colour reproduction. This may include managing a budget.

Sub-editor

The sub-editor's intention is to make the page well-organized so that the reader takes in the information quickly and simply. But in the case of magazines, it is also important to make the page look attractive so that the reader wants to linger over the article. Magazine features can be several thousand words in length and it takes clever use of typography and design to keep the reader's attention, no matter how interesting or informative the article may be. While their main job starts when the copy has been written and assigned to a page, some magazine sub-editors also design pages. On a monthly magazine, sub-editing can be shared by all the magazine's staff.

The sub-editor's main tasks are as follows:

1. They read through the copy on their VDU which has been sent to them electronically by the appropriate section editor. The sub-editor carefully checks it for accuracy, legality, spelling and grammar. If they have any concerns about the factual accuracy of the piece or fear certain sections may be libellous they refer back to the section editor or directly to the writer for clarification. If necessary, the piece may be looked over by a lawyer experienced in media law who may suggest rewording.
2. Once the sub-editor is satisfied that the copy is articulate, accurate and legal, they will cut or expand the length to fit the available space as stipulated by the page layout. As the sub-editor is usually an experienced journalist, they will frequently edit the article themselves. If the article needs expanding or if there is a fear that severe editing might alter the meaning of the text, the writer will be asked to make the necessary amendments.
3. Once the story fits the space, the sub-editor writes a headline, explanatory captions for any images on the page and, where the layout specifies, other text devices such as pull-quotes, where direct speech in the text is extracted and highlighted as a graphic element on the page. It may be enlarged and printed in colour in the centre of the page, for example.

All the above stages may be carried out on screen using the latest computer page design software. Alternatively, where that technology is not available, the sub-editor will draw up a page plan on a piece of paper and instruct the computer to make the appropriate typographical alterations so that when a copy of the story is printed out on special paper designed for pasting-up, it can be slotted onto the page grid accurately. Then the entire page will be prepared in the production phase for printing. However, it is rare for magazines to use this method, especially in the case of consumer titles who expect the highest quality of photographic and text reproduction which can be effectively achieved using up-to-the minute technology.

Sub-editors on magazines need to have a combination of journalistic skills, so they can edit text to a high standard, and creativity, so they can design a visual format for the layout which best conveys the copy. This is especially important in the consumer bracket where visual appeal is vital.

Magazine writers

This category of employee encompasses many personnel hired or commissioned for a variety of capacities. For simplicity's sake, they can be subdivided into feature writers and news reporters. While some larger magazines will have writers dedicated to either news or features, many business publications will expect news reporters also to produce regular features. This is because features are often extended, in-depth news articles in business magazines. In contrast, features in consumer magazines, particularly women's magazines or the music press, involve far more creativity in the use of language which is not normally appropriate for industry-related articles. Consumer magazines also have news sections which are devoted to shorter pieces reporting on the latest developments and events relevant to the readership. For example, *New Musical Express* weekly music paper will contain court reports appertaining to, say, a copyright infringement in its news pages.

Feature writers and news reporters may be employed on a staff contract but increasingly these functions are performed by freelance journalists who are paid per article or feature commissioned. (The work of freelance journalists is covered in Chapter 8.) Let us first deal with the tasks and attributes common to both roles, then deal with each job title separately.

Magazine writers have a basic remit to:

1. generate and initiate ideas for articles or working to the brief set by the section editor;

2. carry out research and interviews to gather relevant information for the piece;
3. write copy to the required length, standard and style.

But because distinctions between jobs are more blurred in magazines than, say, in newspapers, writers are required to have an understanding of the overall production of the publication. For example, feature writers on consumer titles will often be required to write headlines and standfirsts (a paragraph standing separate from the text which helps promote it) and read and correct their story once it has been typeset to ensure its accuracy.

Initiating good ideas requires being highly observant and well-read in all that is going on within your particular sector. That means reading the relevant journals and maintaining close contact with your main sources. You also have to keep a clear idea of your audience – what makes them tick, what is going to be relevant and interesting to them at the present time. Idea generation coupled with good writing style are the key attributes looked for by magazines when recruiting writers. It is common practice for candidates applying for magazine jobs to be asked to come up with several article suggestions for that publication.

Ultimately, magazine writers are guided by the same principles and practices as all other journalists when it comes to researching and writing their pieces. These are discussed in detail in Chapter 1.

Feature writers Newspaper features in the previous chapters are very relevant to the work of magazine writers except for one fundamental difference. Whereas the shelf life of a newspaper might be one day, a magazine might be on the newsstands for at least one month which demands that the feature writer devise story ideas with long-term appeal. Readers are less likely to throw away a magazine after they have read it because it is more expensive but also because many of the features do not have a sell-by date. They could be just as topical and interesting if read a year later. Feature writers have four main tasks: idea generation, gathering information, writing copy and considering the visual presentation of their text.

1. **Idea generation** To ensure the long-term appeal of magazines, feature writers have to generate ideas that are not going to be

out-of-date when the magazine is published. Whereas news-papers are compiled only hours before they appear on the streets, magazines are planned months ahead which means the content has to be fairly timeless in its appeal. 'Knowing what will make a good feature is a combination of learned skills and innate ability', according to a features editor working for a women's magazine. 'You have to read all competing publications, gather as much information as possible about your audience so you can tap into areas that stimulate them, and finally use your imagination and experience to develop the facts into creative writing.' When devising a feature idea, the writer will usually have to provide a working title plus an in-depth summary of the key points to be examined and the potential interviewees. This will be given to the section editor either orally or on paper.

Once the idea has been formed, presented to and approved by the appropriate section editor, the writer will be given a word-count and deadline to adhere to. This is also the case if the idea is generated by another source and given as a brief to the writer.

2. Gathering information Feature writing can only be done following in-depth research and interviews. You could have three pages to fill on one subject so you need to read as far and wide as possible on the subject and speak to as many people involved for every perspective. Whereas news reporters have tighter deadlines and are required to work mainly from the office, a feature writer may be given a couple of weeks to produce their piece simply because they may need to travel to gather their material. Magazine interviews can last hours or even be carried out over several days to enable the journalist not only to glean as much of the factual material as is necessary to span several thousand words of copy, but also to get to 'know' their interviewee. This is especially important when writing a biographical piece such as the type found in the supplements to quality Sunday newspapers.

3. Writing copy As the readership of a magazine may be closely defined, it is vital that feature writers produce copy in a style that is attractive to their audience. For example, while a formal, official tone might be appropriate for a law publication, it would be out of place in a young person's wildlife title. By virtue of their length, magazine features need to be written in a way that will keep the reader's attention for approximately 2500 words. This is achieved in different ways in different magazines. For example, a magazine aimed at parents-to-be will contain lots of reassuring first-hand accounts by new mothers and fathers because they know that real-life experiences will appeal to their apprehensive audience more than columns of advice from the medical profession. An important characteristic that may separate features from news is that the writer may express an opinion and even describe their own experiences if it is relevant to the subject matter, as long as it does not appear biased or in any way infringe media law.

4. Magazine feature writers are usually required to think in terms of the **visual presentation** of their work. For example, they suggest ideas for pictures or graphics and will be required to discuss their suggestions with photographers.

News reporters If the periodical contains a news section, as often happens, the role of reporting and writing shorter, objective factual articles may go to specific individuals or form part of the work of other personnel. News values on a magazine may differ from those of a newspaper in that the editor has to consider carefully what is going to interest their target market. The daily work of a news reporter on a magazine follows the same order as that of a feature writer except that the timescale over which it takes place is shorter. A news reporter may work on several items in one day. News has to be a factual account which means the journalist has to keep their own views out of the story and allow the reader to make up their own mind.

Editorial assistant
Editorial assistants appear more often in the editorial departments of larger consumer titles. In most magazines roles overlap so an editorial assistant is in a good position to learn about all aspects of production as well as writing and earn promotion on their merits. Although this is a typical first job in magazines, there is a great deal of competition for it because of the long-term opportunities it affords. To get in, you have to be a 'jack-of-all-trades', with typing and shorthand skills as well as demonstrable journalistic acumen. As in newspapers, there are a great deal of general administrative duties to be undertaken, from filing to

typing letters to maintaining the office diary; therefore, a lot of physical legwork can be involved. But opportunities often arise for editorial assistants to gain journalistic experience. Editorial assistants' duties include:

1. proofreading and basic writing duties as and when needed;
2. filing, typing letters and other general administrative tasks;
3. liaising with other departments in the magazine on behalf of editorial staff;
4. assisting the editorial staff with research, telephone calls and interviewing if required.

Pictures

Again, it is impossible to generalize about the numbers and titles of photographic staff on magazines and periodicals or their job descriptions. Many magazines have more time than, say, a newspaper, to produce the finished publication and have more scope for using images creatively.

This flexibility leads to different staffing systems based on a variation of a combination of in-house and freelance staff. Magazines have a small team of in-house photographers who will take the majority of pictures. Often freelance photographers who are based in a convenient location to the shoot or have a particular style that would suit the nature of the brief (instructions or summary of requirements) will be commissioned. A magazine is likely to have a picture editor, located within the design or production department of the publication to manage freelance and internal photography. In other circumstances, these functions will be undertaken by the art editor or section editors who have a creative, commissioning and co-ordinating role. But for simplicity, let us refer to a picture editor.

A picture editor will know the best way to creatively illustrate a feature or story, whether it is through graphics or photographs. They may initiate ideas for image-based features or they may interpret the requirements given to them by editorial staff.

The picture editor's commissioning role will be to develop a bank of freelance or in-house photographers or image creators who can best achieve the result they are looking for. Picture editors of leading publications are inundated with portfolios from aspiring and experienced photographers hoping to gain a showcase for their work and picture editors are always looking for new talent who can add a particular dimension to the magazine's creative repertoire.

The picture editor will brief the photographer and agree a deadline and fee according to internal budgetary and time constraints.

The picture editor may be supported by a picture researcher who undertakes administrative duties and assists with the co-ordination of staff and available budget. Part of this co-ordination may involve liaising with picture agencies and archives. These are organizations holding banks of images which are greatly used by magazines. For instance, if a movie magazine is profiling a film actor, as well as pictures they may already have on file, the magazine may require stills from previous performances which they can acquire from picture archives. Agencies, on the other hand, supply new pictures to a specification. The agency will have its own staff photographers or may use freelances who receive a fee. The publication then pays a sum to the agency for its work. Picture researchers need to be visually aware with a keen knowledge of photography. Increasingly, picture researchers are only needed for major projects which require intensive research for rare images. Therefore, they will be hired on a freelance basis as and when they are needed.

That is a breakdown of the key personnel in magazine journalism, but will their roles change in the future?

NEW AND FUTURE DEVELOPMENTS IN MAGAZINE JOURNALISM

The technological revolution in magazines means that today all copy, pictures, graphics and advertisements can be filed onto and accessed via massive computer networks linked to hundreds of visual display unit workstations by hundreds of metres of cabling. Copy is written, inputted, proofread, subbed and laid out on screen without a trace of paper or ink ever hitting anyone's desk. Even photographs can be taken on cameras which need no film but can be hooked up to a computer to give either instant printouts or on-screen images. These can then be retouched, cropped and manipulated in seconds at the push of a button and the drag of a mouse.

However, the computer is no longer a means to an end but a medium in its own right. The CD-Rom publishing market is enjoying a boom. Books, journals, magazines and textbooks are now being produced on a single CD which slots into a special computer Rom drive. In the long term experts predict that we may be able to read our daily diet of news from updatable CD-Rom and already on-line news services are available on subscription through the Internet. The benefits of CD-Rom are that the disks can store vast amounts of information which would present unlimited potential to readers, journalists and advertisers. CD-Rom uses images, text and even sound and moving pictures in an interactive form which, like a newspaper, allows the reader to read at their own pace and choose which pages they want to see in whatever order. Journalists have the opportunity to deliver information in an almost three-dimensional form and advertisers have the scope to create highly evocative imagery for a medium which demands the full attention of the user/reader.

In magazine production, design is of paramount importance and periodicals have tended to set the trends in terms of production innovation and technological trends. The Head of the Periodicals Training Council believes that the design of a publication is what attracts the reader in the first place and the writing is what keeps them there. Many magazine designs and designers are household names even though you may never see their faces, for example Neville Brody and his blueprint for *The Face* in the 1980s.

Consumer magazines are particularly design-oriented with artists and sub-editors often given a free remit over how they treat a page or section. Business publications will tend to have a set format which subs fit into but it is often colourful and innovative. Designs need to be new and fresh and, in magazines in particular, are constantly re-evaluated and renewed. Newspapers are starting to catch on, producing design-conscious supplements and incorporating more white-space and carefully chosen fonts. But with a few exceptions it is magazines which set the pace.

This design-consciousness highlights the need for journalists of the future to think of their work visually as well as through words. The distinction between words and pictures is no longer with us. Text can be used as an aesthetic element and images can tell a story or create a mood as effectively as a long-winded description. It is clear that a new generation of younger readers, who have grown up at ease with staccato images and words thrown at them from computer screens, are going to demand their information in more stylized, innovative ways.

In contrast, those who work in the business-to-business periodical sector believe that is one area where readers might resist dramatic changes in format. Computer databases providing the latest information on mergers, takeovers and new developments are available to subscribers but these services have not threatened the stability of periodicals which may have been published for over a century. It is for that reason that editors in this sector prefer to maintain a familiar format and appearance for their publications. One editor says that while his magazine may keep its current image, the way it is produced will move them into the twenty-first century: 'Many more tasks will be carried out on screen. Photographers will make use of image manipulation software, graphics will be generated by computer. It will change the work of practitioners and could possibly create extra work for them. But the work will be more interesting.'

But what the techno-revolution may do is take away the pleasures we associate with periodicals. Magazines are very much a tactile product as well as a visual product. No-one knows this better than the producers of glossy women's magazines who choose the silkiest paper to produce the softest feel and the best photo reproduction. Advertisers impregnate card pull-outs with perfume to enhance the luxury appeal of the magazine. You can soak in the bath with your copy of *Cosmopolitan*. But you can't with your computer. Yet.

Print journalism: training and entry routes

There are four main ways to get into print journalism:

1. pre-entry courses;
2. by applying direct;
3. transferring from other print media jobs;
4. company training schemes.

This section will be divided into two parts, one each for newspapers and magazines. However, as many magazine journalists have a newspaper training, it is advisable to read the first section even if you wish to go directly into periodicals.

NEWSPAPER TRAINING AND ENTRY ROUTES

Courses

Opportunities for training in print journalism are wide-ranging. From adult education classes or night school to postgraduate study, journalism courses are booming. Many different organizations offer training – you will see them advertising in the national press and it is a good idea to shop around. The types of courses you will encounter are:

- short courses (night classes, weekend or 3-day courses);
- one-year full-time courses;
- two-year HND courses;
- three-year undergraduate degrees;
- one-year postgraduate courses.

Short courses

These are offered by local authorities and private training organizations and you will see them advertised in the media. Students of these courses rarely gain more than an introduction to the work of journalists but they are ideal for those who are considering the profession but want to know more before they commit themselves to a prolonged period of study. Local authority courses do not offer a final qualification (except in the case of a GCSE or A-level in media studies) but they are taught by former or working journalists who equip students with basic writing skills. They are ideal for anyone who is thinking of offering freelance copy to local media as you will be taught how to present your copy correctly.

Weekend and other short-term courses are offered by private training organizations, cost more and provide more intensive training. Some offer an overall introduction to journalism, covering newsroom practice, interviewing and writing where students leave with a small portfolio of their own work. Others concentrate on one particular aspect such as how to write a magazine feature or how to perform a successful interview. These more specific courses are better for journalists who are already trained and who want to brush up on a specific skill rather than for beginners.

One-year pre-entry courses

These are again offered by more than one body. Among the most popular is the National Council for the Training of Journalists (NCTJ) which was founded in 1952 and has been the main organization for the formal training of journalists for more than forty years. There used to be two main ways journalists were appointed and trained via the NCTJ:

1. newspapers appointed trainees who had completed a one-year full-time course at an NCTJ accredited college; or
2. newspapers appointed untrained entrants who would attend a 12-week full-time block-release course within the first year.

Now in addition to those routes, other available options include:

3. entrants attend an NCTJ college one day a week for at least 12 months;

4. entrants are sent on NCTJ one-week courses in Law and Public Affairs and undertake distance learning study.

Let us look first at the one-year pre-entry course, which is run by several universities and colleges yearly. Contact the NCTJ at the address below for an up-to-date list of venues and for details on how to apply.

This is a full-time course taught by experienced journalists where students learn the following:

- law as it affects journalists;

- the operations of local and central government;

- journalistic practice including interviewing, writing and ethics;

- shorthand;

- in some cases basic sub-editing and layout.

Classroom exercises and teaching are supplemented with visits to court, council meetings and role-playing simulations. Halfway through the course, students take Part 1 exams in Law, Public Administration and Journalistic Practice. Part 2 papers are sat at the end. Shorthand may be taken at any point during the year, depending on the candidate's progress.

Fees and living costs may be covered by grants, sponsorships or loans. The college may be able to advise you.

Jobs are not guaranteed after the course. Students are expected to find trainee vacancies on local newspapers where they serve an 18-month on-the-job training period to qualify them for the National Certificate Examination (NCE). Some may be assessed for a National/Scottish Vocational Qualification (NVQ/SVQ) in addition or instead.

Entry qualifications

Two A-level passes and two GCSE or O-level passes. One of the passes at at least one of these levels must be in English. At GCSE or O-level, passes must be grade A, B or C. Or candidates must have successfully completed an NCTJ recognized access course, run by several colleges which exempts the students from normal educational qualifications. Applicants with Scottish educational qualifications must possess at least three Highers, including

English, plus at least two Standard or O grades at levels 1, 2 or 3 in different subjects.

Selection for these courses is quite strict and involves a day of written tests which may or may not lead to interview by a three-strong panel of journalists. Block release courses, which are similar in content, are dealt with later.

Two-year HND courses

These are extended versions of the standard one-year pre-entry courses but entry qualifications and course content varies from college to college, so shop around. These courses contain an academic or theoretical strand, such as examining the content for media messages for bias and looking at the ways audiences or readers react to what they encounter. While there is a strong vocational element, HNDs are not training courses in the same way as the pre-entries. For example, students may not be required to take Part 1 and Part 2 exams, although some might be given the option. Shorthand training might also not be given. Some HNDs contain a short period of work placement at a media organization which is organized by the student in conjunction with tutorial staff.

Degrees

Degrees and media courses
At one time, journalists who had a degree would be sneered at but today, with more opportunities for people to enter higher education, having a degree has almost become a prerequisite for entering the news industry. Employers say it's not down to snobbery – there are good reasons why a graduate possessing the right combination of skills may stand a better chance than someone without a degree.

Like it or not, it's a changing profession which is incorporating the latest technology and working practices. But it is also very traditional and the people at the top, for the moment anyway, tend to place importance on paper qualifications. To editors, a degree shows that you are academically bright and that you have the ability to gather, synthesize and represent information. It's not so much what you studied that bothers editors. There are plenty of journalists who have Bachelor of Arts in Geography,

History, Politics and many with science degrees. A lively, wide-ranging intelligence is what matters, not what you can theorize about which is why a degree is often more symbolic than directly applicable.

Where the subject does matter is if you plan to become a specialist reporter, perhaps working on a scientific issue. There has been a call by editors for graduates with more specialized backgrounds to train in journalism so they can bring their expertise to the media. Another reason why editors prefer graduates to direct entrants is that they believe three years of living away from home and fending for yourself tends to make you more confident and 'worldly'.

Today, nearly every institution in the UK is offering some form of media course in a variety of guises, from night classes in photo-journalism to three-year journalism degrees to joint-honours in English and Communications. The main basis of undergraduate media degrees is the theoretical analysis of texts, from films to advertising. Students examine the impact the media has on our lives and the way it has been achieved. Communication studies courses look at all aspects of communication, from one-to-one human interaction to the mass media.

There is, though, an apparent backlash – with no real explanation – by editors against media-oriented courses. Some editors may feel journalists who are well-read in media criticism may lead them to question editorial policy, so do not think having such a qualification will automatically give you a head start. Many employers genuinely believe that students should gain a wide knowledge while studying and not be too narrowly-focused. Institutions offering media studies have responded to the implied need and to the prejudice against purely theoretical courses by offering syllabuses which incorporate an element of vocational training. Students learn the rudiments of journalism, print, video and sound production and many undertake a lengthy placement in the industry.

It is feared that there are too many media graduates leaving college and university but not enough jobs in the media to accommodate them. However, recruitment evidence suggests that media degrees are responding to the needs of the industry and the tide of suspicion is changing. And not all media students want to work in the industry but have aspirations in education or interests in the theoretical dimensions of their course.

The editorial training and development manager of IPC Magazines is supportive of vocationally based media degrees. She says her organization takes students, and sometimes their tutors, from these degrees on work placements and they do tend to be one-step ahead of their peers and bring useful skills with them. Other people in the print industry agree. One newspaper editor believes the actual degree subject does not matter. He has no objections to media degrees and feels a vocational course of study is as beneficial as spending three years reading history. If you are thinking of applying for a media studies degree with a view to becoming a practitioner, however, examine the course prospectus carefully and always endeavour to meet the teaching staff and ask them whether they have industry experience or close links with the media before taking up a place.

Whatever subject you decide on, be it astrophysics or fine art, be prepared to be a journalist from day one. When the university and college societies start recruiting freshers, make a beeline for the magazine or newspaper and get yourself on the list and ideally on the editorial committee.

The *UCAS Handbook* is a directory of degree courses which can be found in careers offices and libraries which will give you more detail. Journalism, media studies and communications degrees are primarily an academic qualification, not a vocational course so you won't obtain NCTJ qualifications. Many of these courses offer a production module which allows students to learn practical journalistic skills. These can be a good stepping stone to a postgraduate vocational course.

Postgraduate courses
These are starting to emerge in various forms including diplomas, MAs and PhDs. The NCTJ has accredited postgraduate diplomas which are largely vocational qualifications. They differ from the pre-entry courses in that they are more intensive and may require additional theoretical assignments. They also contain a placement period in industry. Applicants must have a degree or relevant qualification and/or experience. MAs, which are Masters Degrees, are strictly for graduates and they may be taught or research-based over one or two years. Content varies but they look at journalism from historical, cultural and sociological perspectives. Some MAs offer vocational training

and/or business practice. All require an extended essay or dissertation of an academic nature researched and presented by the student. PhDs are at the top of the academic scale and are research-based studies lasting from three years upwards. Applicants must have a degree and usually an MA plus a research hypothesis they wish to investigate. PhDs are not traditional routes into journalism.

Applying direct

This is a popular route into a first journalism job and you should refer to Chapter 9 for details on how to do this. Candidates who can demonstrate commitment and enthusiasm with an ability to learn even with limited prior journalistic experience will be considered for a job. In this case, the newspaper may send the applicant for post-entry training. Where this occurs, direct entrants to newspapers serve a probationary period in-house and undertake the foundation course of distance learning. After six months they can attend a college-based 12-week block-release course at one of several colleges in the UK.

Entry qualifications

- five passes in grades A, B or C at GCSE or O-level (or equivalent in another public examination); or

- one A-level pass plus a further four GCSE or O-level passes (or equivalent public examination) in different subjects; or

- two A-level passes plus a further two GCSEs or O-levels (or equivalent) in different subjects.

Transferring from other print media jobs

Secretaries, advertising representatives and others have found their way into journalism by design or by accident. Many employers are impressed by applicants who know the organization in depth. Someone who already works for the newspaper will have advance warning of when journalistic vacancies will be arising which enables them to have a head start over external applicants.

Company training schemes

A number of newspapers appoint new journalists to their own training schemes. This is done on the basis of a fixed-term contract lasting around two years during which time the candidate undertakes on-the-job training and short courses. This may be in the context of the National Vocation Qualification scheme which is described in detail later on. Content varies but during the scheme, trainees learn about media law, public administration, journalistic practice, layout and sub-editing. They will also learn about other non-editorial departments such as advertising. For example, **Liverpool Daily Post and Echo Ltd** has a structured graduate trainee scheme taking on two or three applicants every September for a two-year training period and undertakes to employ them as staff before their two years are up. The company has an arrangement with Thomson, a large regional newspaper group, and Post and Echo trainees go to Newcastle for four months' formal training and spend the rest of their time in Liverpool working in news, sub-editing, sport, features and a period in circulation and advertising sales. The trainees take an exam at the end of the Thomson course.

At **News International,** *The Times* runs a scheme to train four graduates a year and the *Sunday Times* has a scheme to train four students in journalism over a three-year period. More than 300 school and college students and university graduates are also accepted every year on a wide variety of work experience programmes.

EMAP plc is one of Britain's major newspaper publishers along with consumer and business magazines. Its chain of titles includes daily regional newspapers and a network of paid-for and free-distribution weeklies with a combined circulation of more than 2.4 million. It runs a two-and-a-half year training scheme for its newspaper recruits which is partly in-house and partly at the company's own training centre. If you join an EMAP newspaper, you will undertake 20 weeks of intensive training at a residential training centre in Peterborough. During this time, candidates are taught 100 wpm shorthand, news writing, basic photography, media law and public administration. Training also entails real-life exercises such as attending court cases, press conferences and covering council meetings. Trainees are expected to go out and find stories then desktop publish them back in the office. After completing the course, the next two years involve further in-house training and regular assessment until qualifying for the EMAP Diploma in Journalism.

Entry qualifications
Ideally, you will have five GCSE or equivalent passes at grades A–C and preferably at least two A-levels. At least one pass at GCSE level should be in English.

Funding
EMAP newspapers finance the training of new recruits they send to the training centre but they do take private students provided the centre thinks they are suitable and that they understand that there is no guarantee of a job at the end of their training. EMAP, Training Centre, 57 Priestgate, Peterborough, PE1 1JW, tel: 01733 892444.

Training schemes do not automatically guarantee a job at the end of the period but the majority of candidates are kept on. This is not an exhaustive list of training schemes and you are advised to contact newspapers directly to see if they run their own.

Assessment and examinations

For the past forty years, NCTJ students undertook one single national assessment where, if they passed, they gained an NCTJ Proficiency Certificate in Newspaper Journalism. But now there are options, for example, a prospective journalist can now take the National Certificate Examination (NCE) in journalism (former Proficiency Certificate) and the comparatively new National and Scottish Vocation Qualifications (S/NVQs) introduced by the Government.

What is the difference between the NCE and S/NVQ?
NCE: NCTJ holds twice-yearly exams at ten universities, Birmingham, Cambridge, Exeter, Kent, Lancaster, London, Newcastle, Sheffield, Southampton and Strathclyde. To qualify for the exam, trainees must have passed seven compulsory preliminary examinations – Newspaper Journalism, Handout exercise, Law parts 1 and 2, Public Administration parts 1 and 2 and Shorthand at 100 wpm. These exams will usually have been

taken at their training college or centre.The exam is held in the Spring and Autumn and is currently broken down into four main sections but the NCTJ is proposing changes to the format:

1. Face-to-face interview with telephone follow-through to produce a story. Candidates interview someone, such as a police officer, in a role-play situation. They then return to their desk and follow up the face-to-face conversation with a telephone call to another relevant role-playing contact, such as a fire brigade official, then write a news story based on these interviews. Students are assessed both on their interviewing skills, which are witnessed by an examiner, and writing ability.
2. Speech reporting, write-up and follow-up ideas. A role-playing spokesperson gives a short speech, lasting approximately 10–20 minutes during which the candidate takes notes. Then the journalist must write a story from their notes under exam conditions and suggest other potential stories arising from the content of the speech.
3. News story, based on information obtained from several sources. Candidates are given sheets of paper with quoted speech from various witnesses to an incident plus a few paragraphs of factual detail. This is an exercise in establishing the accurate facts from conflicting statements and reporting speech without contravening media law.
4. Newspaper practice, a test of the candidate's ability to cope with everyday matters arising in the office, covering courts and local and central government.

S/NVQs: Scottish/National Vocational Qualifications sets standards of performance and frameworks for assessing them in newspaper journalism. Standards have been set by the Newspaper Society which is working as a joint awarding body with the Royal Society for the Encouragement of Arts, Manufactures and Commerce (RSA). This system is based on on-the-job assessments by senior staff who certify whether you have achieved a set level of competence. Progress is monitored over a length of time by continuous assessment by either internally appointed assessors (news editors etc.) or by external assessors.

Of course not all would-be journalists know whether the newspaper they will end up working for uses the NCE or NVQ/SVQ route. So what's the point of taking the time and expense of doing seven preliminary NCTJ exams when your paper may use an entirely different in-house training system? The answer is simple: NCE preliminary exams count towards the full assessment of knowledge required to achieve an S/NVQ. Some newspapers using the S/NVQ system require their journalists to undergo a final examination in addition to their continual assessment. This exam varies in content but is a basic test of newsgathering and writing but not on the scale of the NCE.

Shorthand

As well as its own shorthand examinations, the NCTJ accepts 100 words a minute certification from: RSA, Teeline Education Ltd, Pitman College, London Chamber of Commerce and Industry and SCOTVEC.

For more information, contact the NCTJ, Latton Bush Centre, Southern Way, Harlow, Essex CM18 7BL.

PRESS PHOTOGRAPHY: TRAINING AND ENTRY ROUTES

There is a small annual intake of press photographers into this highly competitive part of the industry with two main routes into a newspaper if you are hoping for a staff job.

1. By applying directly to a local paper and hoping to be taken on on the strengths of a good portfolio.
2. By taking a one-year full-time press photography course such as the one at Stradbroke College, Sheffield. At the time of writing, that is the only industry-approved training centre for press photographers in the UK. On this type of course you will learn all you need to know about the job, from the technicalities of using equipment to operating within the law. A major part is devoted to news and journalism so students learn what type of picture is suitable for publication.

Other photography courses at different levels exist throughout the UK which may have an element of journalistic or documentary work within them. Picture editors do not just look for traditional documentary photographers, though, and depending on the publication, they may want something different. This is particularly the case with magazines. Many top fashion photographers started as assistants and worked their way up.

MAGAZINE JOURNALISM:
TRAINING AND ENTRY ROUTES

By their diverse nature, magazines offer a myriad of opportunities. There is a periodical catering for just about every interest or issue and it would seem that publishers are keen to attract recruits reflecting that inherent multiplicity. From eager trainees to enthusiastic amateurs, with perseverance and the right skills and approach, it is possible to get something in print. For those seeking a career in magazines, it is highly graduate-oriented. The degree you take is largely immaterial but there appears to be a dearth in people with strong technical backgrounds who can write with a specialist knowledge. Publishers are anxious to recruit intake from the professions – good news for those who fancy a change of career – who can be trained in the necessary editorial skills. Periodicals also offer many part-time and freelance opportunities. The bulk of copy is commissioned from outside writers. This offers great scope for those men and women who may want to treat journalism as a sideline or who want to combine working with family life.

Pre-entry courses

Routes into magazine journalism are much the same as newspapers so many candidates take an NCTJ course. The NCTJ also offers NVQs in Periodical Journalism. Contact them at the address above for further details. Alternatively, the Periodicals Training Council, which is the training body overseeing the magazine industry, has accredited several courses offering vocational magazine training. An up-to-date list can be obtained from the Periodicals Training Council, 15–19 Kingsway, London, WC2B 6UN.

Courses vary in length and content but address the following areas:

- journalistic practices;
- media law;
- feature writing;
- layout and design.

Refer to the section on newspaper training above about short courses, degrees and postgraduate qualifications as the same information applies to magazine training opportunities.

Company training schemes

Many companies, at one time, had excellent in-house training schemes where recruits were launched into their journalistic careers from day one and had good prospects for future development. Now few organizations offer in-house training but more and more, particularly with the encouragement of the Periodicals Training Council, are becoming their own assessment centres for NVQS. The benefits of training on-the-job are obvious. Working alongside experienced journalists, meeting real deadlines, covering real stories in the context of your own publication are all going to rub off. Plus you get paid and magazine wages are usually better for a first-timer than newspapers. For example, at **IPC** the training period for new entrants usually takes two years. In that time, they will be trained in the rudiments of law, subediting, production and printing skills, layout and design, researching, writing and interviewing. Editors act as mentors and will tick off in a log-book as the trainee achieves particular standards in set tasks.

In-house training is obviously beneficial to the entrant in giving them a very broad approach to periodical production, from writing, to layout to production. From IPC's point of view, it is beneficial in ensuring that standards are met and that trainees get to know their publication's house-style intimately. IPC also offers training in the longer term for employees to update their skills in editorial, legal and technological matters.

When applying for magazine training schemes, how do you compete against the other hopefuls who have the same experience and qualifications as you? Here are a few pointers for success from the Periodicals Training Council:

1. If you have a technical skill, interest or qualification, promote it. There appears to be a dearth of technically qualified journalists and specialist publications are actively seeking people from the professions to apply. This is good news for late entrants. Whereas other media appear to prefer younger candidates, magazines often welcome people who have experience elsewhere and want to shift their attentions to writing about it. The Periodicals Training Council recently presented a Young Journalist of the Year award to a 39-year-old specialist writer.

2. Research the publication you are aiming for so that you can demonstrate in-depth knowledge of its style and market.
3. Following on from this, go armed with ideas which reflect your research.
4. Your application must be immaculate – you are dealing with a highly design-conscious communications industry so attention to detail is essential.

Good luck.

5

Radio

Radio has been described as blind by some critics who claim that its reliance on sound and lack of pictorial accompaniment, either still or moving, makes it inferior as a journalistic medium. But others, and not just those who choose to work within radio, believe it is the best and purest way of mediating news and current affairs. It's fast, immediate and stimulates the imagination and senses not tested by print or television.

With its range of voices, sounds and effects, at its best, radio can evoke a picture more vivid than might be achieved on paper or screen. Whereas newspaper pages are subbed and camera shots framed, radio has the ability to impart information without obvious intrusion. Radio journalists claim the pieces they produce are more factual and unbiased due as much to time constraints on production as to stricter laws over what the medium can broadcast. The sheer portability of radio means you can listen to it anywhere and it leaves you free to do other activities at the same time. It follows, therefore, that radio has tremendous immediacy as a journalistic medium.There is no need for pictures or film to support the story. If an event is unfolding during transmission, a journalist can break into a programme at that moment and talk to the audience about it. One station's Head of News and Sport says of radio: 'It's probably the purest form of news we've got.' However, it's not totally 'pure' because, when handling a story, radio journalists must decide what the top line, or main focus, of an event is. For example, if employees walk out on strike then that will be reported over the fact that there has been a grievance at this firm for two years.

For documentaries, which are another important aspect of radio journalism, the medium offers the reporter tremendous scope for imaginative, creative use of sound to convey full and detailed information on an issue.

In this chapter, we will discover more about radio's impact as a journalistic medium by examining the roles of those who work in radio journalism. We will also look at how stories are gathered and produced for broadcast over the airwaves. But first, here is a guide to the way the radio industry looks today.

THE SHAPE OF THE RADIO INDUSTRY

According to figures from the National Council for the Training of Broadcast Journalists, the broadcast industry as a whole is actually quite small. There are probably less than 5000 full-time broadcast journalists operating in the whole of the United Kingdom. That figure covers all those working in radio and television in the BBC and the independent sector, satellite broadcasting and specialist production companies. The UK's radio provision is made up of national and regional services provided by the BBC and independent local radio (ILR) stations. New independent national channels, such as Classic FM, Virgin 1215 and Talk Radio UK have also recently reached the airwaves.

News gathering, production and output for broadcasting is becoming increasingly bi-media organized which means journalists are working for both radio and television and it is inevitable that the structural distinctions between the two areas will become more blurred.

The BBC is Britain's public service broadcaster and began daily radio broadcasts in Britain in 1922. According to its first Director General, John Reith, the BBC was to be run as a public service, to inform and educate on all that is best in human endeavour, knowledge and achievement. Funded through the licence fee, the BBC's independence is guaranteed by its status as neither a government department nor a commercial company. It operates under a Royal Charter which requires it to broadcast educational, informational and entertainment services. Its charter which expired in 1996 has been renewed for another 10 years.

The BBC provides five national radio channels (1, 2, 3, 4 and 5 Live) and a network of 39 local radio stations. Local BBC stations have their own newsrooms and also provide material for the national network to ensure regional coverage on national bulletins.

The BBC also delivers radio and television programmes to a global audience through BBC World Service. The radio strand of the World Service is partly funded through a Parliamentary grant which for 1994/5 totalled £175m. The BBC is headed by a Board of twelve Governors whose responsibility is to ensure the corporation meets its role as a public service broadcaster and maintains standards. They are appointed normally for five years by the Queen in Council. The day-to-day running of the corporation is performed by the Director-General who is appointed by the Board.

The BBC held a monopoly in radio broadcasting between 1926 and 1954, suiting Reith's notion that unified control was essential to maintaining high standards. But his aim to raise cultural and educational standards of the nation became unpopular in some quarters, especially on Sundays when listeners were fed a heavy diet of serious music and religious affairs. From the 1930s, listeners began to pick up popular commercial programmes broadcast by Radio Luxembourg and pirate Radio Caroline, creating competition for the BBC. But it wasn't until the 1972 Sound Broadcasting Act that commercial radio was finally legalized, nearly 20 years after the introduction of commercial television. The change was a result of pressure by MPs and a lobby of advertisers, the former anxious to lessen the political influence of the BBC and the latter to find an outlet for promoting their products. But the ideology behind the move was that it would extend the freedom of choice to the listener.

Today, there are approximately 140 independent local radio services. The word 'services', as opposed to stations, is important here because some stations provide two or more different services, with a completely different character and audience, on the FM and AM bands. Many more are likely to be cropping up as the Radio Authority, which oversees radio output, has been inviting bids for new local franchises. Some cities, which are currently served by a BBC local and ILR service, may before too long be offered an all-news service, music station and community broadcasting service.

Most ILR stations have their own newsrooms but may opt-out in the evening and at weekends when bulletins are provided by the agency Independent Radio News and Reuters Radio, a new rival service.

Local radio is the main starting point for most radio journalists. These teams are small and close-knit. Newsrooms are on

the whole characterized by their friendly atmosphere and cama-
raderie as they are staffed by young and largely ambitious
reporters eager to work to their highest capabilities, although this
can also lead to competition for the best stories. Whereas the BBC
will take on trainees with little or no previous experience, it is
harder for the beginner to break into ILR stations, which are predominantly music-based and have little news air-time. They
prefer their intake to be experienced in radio, print or at least to
have completed a postgraduate pre-entry course in radio journalism so that they come armed with some journalistic and
technical skills.

BBC local radio has a mandate to be the people's station in the
area they serve. When they first started, local organizations such
as angling clubs were invited in to do their own programmes.
With growing competition from commercial stations BBC stations started playing more music. Now they are tending to go the
other way again, incorporating more speech-based programming, news and current affairs. Rather than compete in terms of
music, local BBC stations concentrate on trying to provide a distinctive, local feel to their output, talking more about the community. They often serve a similar service, and have a compara-
ble identity, to a local or regional newspaper with their commitment to local news. Regular 'phone-in programmes are akin to
newspaper letters pages and popular columnists are encouraged
to host programmes.

ILR stations primarily provide music and entertainment. FM
stations generally aim for a younger audience, playing pop
music around the clock. Most have hourly, two- or three-minute
news bulletins with slightly longer news programmes at peak-
times. These may be interspersed with headlines every 20
minutes at breakfast and drive-time which is around 4pm to
6pm. The AM services of ILR stations, which plays so-called
'gold' music for a 35-plus audience, again offer entertainment-
based music and chat for the most part but may have slightly
longer news bulletins. There is a fierce battle for listeners between
local BBC stations and ILRs with AM services trying to cut into
the opposition's audiences. It is an anxious time for station managers whenever the latest listening figures are published.

Radio news is a 24-hour operation and the work is fast and
furious when faced with yards of tape to edit in time for your
hourly bulletin. Working hours can be infuriating with overnight

shifts and early morning starts a regular part of the job. If there is a story to be covered you cannot go home midway and leave someone else to edit your tape for you. You may have to stay till the bitter end. Documentaries may be the culmination of lengthy research and production yet they are often only finalized minutes before broadcast to ensure the information contained within them is as up to date as possible. This can be very nerve-racking. For instance, what if the 'Mr Big' you have interviewed for your 45-minute-long programme on drug smuggling is suddenly arrested? Will your documentary have to be quickly re-edited to avoid breaching the laws of contempt? Or worse, will it be cancelled?

On the plus side, there is plenty of opportunity to hear your work broadcast nationally, whether you work for the BBC or ILR. BBC will use items from the regions and ILR reporters can feed material to IRN and Reuters Radio.

The newsroom set-up and the work of radio journalists does tend to differ in ILR and the BBC. ILR journalists are encouraged to be first with the news and to work around hourly bulletins. They produce shorter reports than the BBC and are less likely to produce longer packages or documentaries. Conversely, BBC has far more airtime devoted to news and therefore radio journalists have far more scope for elaborate, creative pieces.

BBC National Radio

Output at BBC radio at a network level is divided into a number of sections or disciplines:

1. News programmes

Various news programmes are prepared throughout the day. Some items are planned well-ahead but much of the output has to be in response to the big issues of the day. The content of the programme is discussed at an editorial conference and journalists are allocated a story to prepare.

2. Radio newsroom

Journalists working in the radio newsroom produce summaries for Radios 1, 2, 3 and 4 and 5 Live as well as operating a general news service for the regions.

3. Specialist programmes

Staff work towards output for business in particular as well as providing stories for the general news programmes and bulletins.

4. Weekly programmes and features

Weekly programmes give in-depth, detailed commentary and analysis of current issues. Here staff work in very small teams, originating and developing features which expand and explain the background behind the news. This is the area of documentary-making many journalists aspire to. Teams may spend months researching and preparing their programmes.

5. Journalists in the regions

BBC News and Current Affairs has a remit to cover the whole of the UK, particularly on Radio 5 Live which has dedicated journalists working on news coverage on the network in twelve regional centres. Their brief is to ensure key issues affecting their area are broadcast on the network. The regional centres are: Belfast, Birmingham, Bristol, Cardiff, Glasgow, Leeds, Manchester, Norwich, Nottingham, Plymouth and Southampton.

Commercial radio: national service

Most independent local radio stations are linked to a central organization (Independent Radio News or IRN) which supplies national and international news. IRN employs reporters based in London, ready to be sent anywhere in the country or abroad when a story breaks. Other jobs are deskbound. A reader-writer helps write introductions (cues) then presents them in bulletins, another term for short programmes. The duty producer is responsible for putting bulletins together using editorial judgments to decide the running order of the stories. The duty editor leads the newsdesk team, deciding which stories get covered and how they're presented.

Another key post is the intake editor. This person is constantly on the look-out for stories, monitoring national and international sources of information through the computer and taking calls from stations offering stories. When a story breaks, the intake editor acts instantly. This may mean getting a reporter at a local station to file a report, phoning someone connected with the story direct or dispatching a reporter to the scene.

When journalists in the regions go home their stations can take IRN bulletins through the night. IRN also offers stations in the independent sector specialized sport and financial services.

There are advantages and disadvantages to working in public or commercial broadcasting. One news editor confesses he was apprehensive about his news judgment being threatened by commercial pressures when he left public broadcasting. He says:

> One thing that did bother me before joining commercial radio is that I was very wary that the advertising department might say 'You can't carry that knocking [critical] story about this company because they advertise with us.' In all the time I've been in commercial radio, that's never ever happened, in fact the opposite is true. If we do a knocking story about a high-profile advertiser, the adverts will probably be pulled.

However, with usually only three minutes to fill every hour, journalists working in commercial radio rarely get the chance to do any sort of in-depth reporting or investigative journalism. It is rare to hear a documentary broadcast on commercial radio although some stations do sporadically run half-hour programmes devoted to an issue currently of concern within their catchment area. Where this happens, a news reporter will be assigned to produce the documentary and they will be relieved of some of their general reporting duties as they do it.

At a local and network level, many stations have a bi-media policy for new intake and trainees. This means journalists work for both radio and television. The aim is flexibility and multi-skilling although many would argue that radio and television are very separate media with different production values which are not easily transferable.

The Editor of IRN came into radio after working in newspapers and magazines and believes radio's appeal to journalists lies in its fast pace and the control reporters have over what they produce: 'If you love reporting, the speed at which you can turn around a story holds a special appeal.' He continues that not many others will be involved in the production of your story, giving the journalist relative autonomy. 'I found the thrill of radio was that I could control the story from beginning to end and the fact that once you write a story in the morning, by lunchtime who knows how many people are aware of it.'

Journalists may say that news is news but in radio there are many different ways of presenting the information from a 10-second voice report to a half-hour documentary programme.

How radio journalists treat stories

In the same way as a newspaper journalist, a radio reporter is sent out with the tools of their trade, pen, paper and a portable recorder to gather information. But they also have to consider the added dimension of sound. Sometimes journalists are working in a controlled environment such as a news conference where they are only likely to be able to record voices. In the case of a serious story such as a murder, only voices of, say, the police, eye-witnesses, relatives and the journalist themself would seem appropriate. Other sounds would seem out-of-place. In other situations, such as a demonstration, it's usual to try to convey some of the atmosphere as a backdrop to the facts of the report. So a radio reporter will have to assess what kind of sounds they will need to record to convey the mood of their report as well as gather on paper the facts of the story.

In this section we will examine the variety of ways the journalist might present their story, and in what circumstances it would be appropriate, including;

- newsflash
- teaser
- highlight
- copy story
- voicer
- live report
- wrap
- package

To illustrate each method, we will use a hypothetical story at a commercial station:

It's ten-past-one in the afternoon and the news editor, Susan Smith, has answered a call from a motorist speaking on a mobile telephone who has just witnessed part of a motorway bridge collapsing. She elicits as much detail as she can from the distressed caller who can only confirm the time, location and the current chaotic scenes. The news editor alerts her three strong reporting team who are based in the office and assigns each to call either the fire brigade, ambulance crew and transport police. Meanwhile, the news editor herself calls the local police press office who can only give sketchy details. The reporting team is fighting other media organizations, who have caught wind of the story, for access to information on limited switchboard lines. Susan must however bash out a few lines on her typewriter for immediate broadcast as a **newflash:**

Reports are coming in of a motorway bridge collapse on the outskirts of Manchester. Emergency services are at the scene ... but aren't yet able to give details. One eyewitness has told Manchester News a whole section of the M60 elevated section at Fulwood has plunged into the river below. We'll bring you more on this as we get it.

She dashes to the studio where the current presenter is on air and alerts him to the story. He fades the record he is playing and introduces Susan to the audience:

We must break into this record for an important newsflash ...

Meanwhile, in the newsroom, the editorial assistant is trying to field calls from anxious relatives while the reporters broaden their inquiries to hospitals, the Highways Agency, even neighbouring landowners while they scan their rival stations. It is now 1.25pm, just five minutes before the **highlights.** (A highlight is a short summary of less than fifty words of the main stories which many stations broadcast at half past the hour.) Susan decides the scale of the story merits breaking with convention and running a full story at half-past. Each of the reporters has by now typed a short summary of the information they have gathered which they have handed to the news editor to help her compile her story which reads ...

A motorway bridge on the outskirts of Manchester has collapsed ... plunging vehicles fifty feet into a river below. A major emergency operation's underway at Fulwood Brook to try to find survivors in the water. Eyewitnesses report chaot-

> *ic scenes. It's not yet clear how many vehicles were on the elevated section at the time it collapsed ... but an ambulance spokesman says dozens of cars and lorries could have fallen.*
>
> *Other news now ... schoolteachers are threatening to strike over growing class sizes. They claim standards are suffering and pupils are the hardest hit.*

This first highlight could more accurately be described as a **copy story** which is an extended version of the highlight but without any accompanying actuality (the term given to describe recorded or live material inserted into reports such as interviews). Copy stories last no more than 30 seconds in most news programmes and are used when first reports are coming in and there has not yet been an opportunity to broadcast actuality or when there is not enough time to run a more detailed report. By this stage, rival stations will be competing to broadcast first reports from the scene. Typically, this will come as a **voicer.**

> Susan has dispatched one reporter to the scene in the radio car (a portable radio studio which allows the journalist to transmit quality audio back to the station from any location).

Filing

All journalists have to deliver their reports in time for deadlines and radio journalists are under great pressure not only to provide words but also sounds for use in bulletins. Newspaper journalists will often have to file lengthy, detailed reports down crackly telephone lines to awaiting copytakers and the same is true for radio people. While the amount of words they may use is limited, they also have to find ways of getting sound which is of high enough quality for broadcast to their studio. This can be achieved in several ways if a journalist is out on location:

1. **Telephones** Radio reporters may carry mobile 'phones although in many cases they use public boxes to dictate their report to a colleague in the studio who types it. Or they may

record the reporter's voice. This is especially good if they are calling from the scene of an event and you can hear the atmosphere around them. If the journalist is in a telephone box in the midst of a riot, that is exactly the time they would be expected to file their report rather than finding a quiet place away from the activity.

2. **Radio car** This is a car fitted with a transmitter, microphone and headphones allowing reporters to transmit quality audio back to the studio. As soon as it's obvious a major story has broken a reporter will be sent out in the radio car to gather material. Even on a slow news day the radio car's still very useful. A reporter could, for example, talk to a councillor live on the breakfast show from the scene of a controversial proposed quarry site.

3. **Integrated Services Digital Network (ISDN Lines)** This is a relatively new system used mainly by large stations which enables them to treat quality audio transfer just like a telephone call. The cost of setting up an ISDN link means it tends to be used only for big stories, such as major sporting events where the journalist will be on location for several days or weeks.

As well as filing words and interviews back to the studio, journalists will often transmit wildtrack, that is, a few minutes of appropriate background noise, such as bottles clanking if it's a story about a milk deliverer, or supermarket sounds if it's about a checkout operator winning the pools. This can then be mixed in the studio behind the words to give the report a three-dimensional quality which makes it more interesting to the listener.

Of course there are many other contexts in which stories are put together. It might be researched, edited and filed within the studio, or researched on location and edited and filed at the studio. The journalist may have had to file from location for a bulletin, but they may have to follow the story up once they get back. This may involve producing a longer report – such as a **wrap** or a **package** – for broadcast in the next bulletin or programme.

Meanwhile in our scenario the other reporters in the office are trying to record interviews with emergency service officials over the telephone in a special studio.

Interviewing

A radio journalist's interviewing skills have to be excellent as questions must be phrased in such a way as to elicit the most full and interesting reply from the interviewee for broadcast. That does not mean you put words in the interviewee's mouth, but you do need them to express themselves in a way that sounds good on the radio. Radio interviews will take place either face-to-face or over the telephone.

It's often a good idea to chat informally with more nervous interviewees about what areas you want to cover. This helps put them at ease and enables the reporter to get clear, thought-out responses. When dealing with politicians, though, give nothing away. Often the best material is captured on tape when they're caught off guard. This doesn't happen often, and careful thought preparing questions to get the answers you want is vital.

The radio reporter finds him or herself in a variety of interview situations every day, from the studio telephone talking to a local person caught up in trouble abroad to the steps of a court where a crash victim's won huge damages to a street where angry residents have blocked a road in protest at the danger from speeding motorists. This variety, plus not knowing what might crop up next, is an essential part of the joy of reporting and compensates for working long, unpredictable hours.

A senior journalist at IRN says: 'People can be nervous about the microphone so you have to establish eye contact and make the person feel they are chatting with you rather than the mic. I try to keep the mic well out of the way initially, to build up a rapport. Once the person feels more at ease, I will begin the interview.' It is therefore essential to have good personal interaction skills for reporting. Our journalist explains: 'It is very important to know when to be sympathetic, for instance, if you are sent to the scene of a murder, you should not go up to someone in the street and wave a microphone under their nose. That is just insensitive.'

Telephone interviews, where the reporter records the conversation in a studio, are more difficult because unless the interviewee is experienced, they may be nervous about being recorded and could hang up. The journalist is unable to fall back on eye contact and body language to make the interviewee feel at ease so must compensate with a friendly voice and encouraging words. For example, a caller's phoned the newsroom about hearing an explosion. While you're talking it's confirmed a chemical plant's gone up in smoke. Callers often don't see themselves as eye-witnesses and feel what they've got to say isn't important, when of course with a deadline looming talking to someone even indirectly connected with what's happened can be a major coup in the response battle between stations.

It's important to tell a caller when they're being recorded. By telling the caller that what they've heard **is** important, and asking them to repeat what's just been said, the reporter often gets the report they're after. Keeping things conversational definitely helps as no-one likes to feel pressured.

With five minutes to go to the hour, Susan still does not have any interviews to play so she asks one of the reporters to 'voice' a report which means a reporter other than the news-reader can be heard recounting the story.

This adds interest and immediacy to the programme. The reporter writes just two or three paragraphs on their typewriter so the voicer lasts usually no longer than 30 seconds. Reporters use their judgment and experience to write the correct number of words; they then find a free studio and take in their report and a cart (a loop of tape inside a plastic cartridge upon which the voicer is recorded), first ensuring it has been bulk erased. It is reusable so it must be erased in case any of the previous story can be heard 'underneath' the new report. The bulk eraser instantly removes the magnetic information on the tape which renders it blank again.

In the studio the reporter has two recording options. If there's time he or she can open the microphone and record on to reel-to-reel tape before transferring it to cart. This enables the reporter to make more than one attempt at recording the report. If a dead-line's just minutes away the experienced reporter will record straight onto cart, which will then be whisked away to the bulletin booth ready for broadcast. If time's really short a reporter can end up reading the report live into the bulletin by reading into a second microphone in the booth. A cool head's crucial and when things go well close deadlines provide another big thrill of the job.

> With just seconds to go before transmission, the reporter must write a cue for the presenter which is a paragraph's introduction for them to read out before playing the cart. The cue will read:
>
> *An elevated section of the M60 on the outskirts of Manchester has collapsed into a river killing at least fifteen people. From the scene – Georgina Trent ...*

The reporter will have added the name of the cart, how long the voicer lasts and the **outcue** which is the last couple of words on the cart so the newsreader will know when the cart is finishing to avoid any uncomfortable pauses in the broadcast.

> Susan goes into the studio or small booth from where she will be reading the news programme with a collection of carts and cues. At local radio level bulletins are mainly self-driven. This means she does the technical side of the broadcast as well as the verbal. She's faced by a microphone and controls called faders, which when opened allow her voice and each cart to go out on air. Technical expertise is not required, but mastering the subtleties does take time. Also facing Susan are meters which monitor output levels. Care is needed to avoid the reader's voice sounding louder than the reports she's presenting, but again it's not difficult to get the hang of it.

At the top of the pile of cues are the teasers. These are very brief summaries to the stories coming up which are more abbreviated than the highlights. They are written in the present tense so as to appear immediate and attention-grabbing. For example, the teaser to this story reads:

> *Dozens feared dead in Manchester motorway bridge disaster.*

Newsreading

If you have ever had to listen to yourself on a tape recording or video, you know how self-conscious it can make you feel.

Imagine having to do that ten times a day, knowing that you are being heard by hundreds of thousands or even millions of listeners. To a radio journalist, it's second nature and an important part of their job. You not only have to read bulletins but put your voice to reports and scripts. You may sometimes be called upon to speak spontaneously without a script, for example when you do a two-way interview from the scene of an incident with a studio-based presenter or when you anchor a debate or 'phone-in. Most journalists in a radio newsroom have to learn to be comfortable using their voice as it is one of the tools of their trade. There are roles for radio journalists who work behind the scenes and do not go on air but they are rare. So how do you know if your voice is sufficiently up-to-scratch for a career in radio?

According to one former BBC news editor, the best way of finding out is to sit down with a tape recorder and practise. He said:

> There is a minority of people who just don't sound good on radio. It's nothing to do with accent – people can sing out of tune and some people talk out of tune and can't get out of doing it. One great fault is people 'singing' the news, up and down in exactly the same place in every sentence because they think they are parodying newsreaders.

But these faults can be remedied simply through practice.

As well as being able to speak clearly, calmly and authoritatively, you have to be able to speak to the right speed (which is not something you can pin down to X words-per-minute – it just sounds right) or your bulletins will over-run or end too soon. This, says our news editor, comes with experience: 'You can eventually look at a script and know to within around five seconds how long it is.'

A senior journalist who regularly delivers national bulletins on national network radio, says voice tutoring is not essential but is useful:

> When I was taking my postgraduate diploma at University College Cardiff, a Shakespearean actor came in once a fortnight who helped us to physically deliver our voices. It revolves to a great extent around breathing control and understanding the way our lungs and diaphragm work. If you can learn how to control your breath it helps you deliver powerful, punchy bulletins.

To see what he means, listen to BBC Radio 4 newsreaders and see if you can hear them breathe. You will hear them pause in the right place but not always a breath. When reading the news, you must stay calm and relaxed and slow down. It helps to have an image in your mind of the listener to whom you are reading. The character of your voice also comes through if you sound interested in what you are reading, as long as you don't go over the top.

Meanwhile, the radio car has reached the site of the bridge collapse. The reporter has managed to park close to the cordon and has a good view of the disaster scene. Moments before the hour, he contacted Susan via the talkback mechanism in his radio to say he would be able to provide a live report from the scene during the programme. Through his earpiece, he can hear the programme go on air. Following the teasers, cue and voicer, Susan introduces the reporter and he now goes on air for one minute vividly describing the scene to the audience ...

This is a disaster on a vast scale. Just yards from here I can see the gaping space left when a fifty foot section of the busy M60 collapsed ... plunging dozens of vehicles into the river below. I can tell you police have just confirmed at least twenty bodies have been recovered from the water so far. You can hear the roar of heavy machinery coming from the bank of Fulwood Brook. That's being used to winch cars, vans and lorries from the river. No-one's yet known to have survived the twenty foot fall when the road fell from beneath them. On the jagged edges of the devastated motorway stunned drivers stare in disbelief at the scene of horror before them. The death toll's expected to rise ... and emergency services overwhelmed by the scale of the tragedy are calling in help from neighbouring regions. This is Steve Solo reporting live from Fulwood Brook.

The three o'clock news programme is to be extended to carry a **package** containing recorded interviews interspersed with further live reports and interviews with guests who have been called into the studio.

A package is more common in BBC news and current affairs broadcasts because breakfast and evening drive-time shows are based around extended reports with more detail and alternative angles. Unlike a report for a news bulletin, it gives the reporter more scope to expand and explain. It may last between three and four minutes and contains many more pieces of actuality. A documentary, which may last up to an hour, is in effect an expanded package but the journalist can employ more creative use of sound to make the programme more compulsive listening. Whether they are creating a package or documentary, the journalist has to employ production skills appropriate to the nature of the story. If it is a serious issue, they would be unlikely to use sound effects or music. But on a more human interest story, they can be highly innovative and creative using the full range of their editing and mixing skills.

There are two ways of editing tape depending on what system the station uses. If the station still uses the traditional quarter-inch tape system, the journalist physically edits the tape by cutting it with a razor blade and tapes it to the following section. This method will also be used to edit our pauses in speech, coughs and other elements which hinder the flow of a piece. The alternative method which is growing in popularity is digital editing where the information is stored on computer disk instead of tape. The sound is copied from the main disk to the disk which will be played in the bulletin.

> Meanwhile, as the day progresses and all that is left at the scene is debris while accident investigators try to establish the cause of the tragedy, the tone of later news programme's coverage is changing. There is more analysis to consider why it happened and what can be done to prevent it happening again. And was anyone to blame? By this stage, the events of the day can be condensed into a **wrap**.

A wrap is shorter than a package and may vary in length between 30 to 40 seconds depending on whether it for broadcast on ILR or BBC bulletins. It is usually introduced by a **cue** read by the presenter or newsreader which is a short introduction or summary of the story. The wrap itself usually consists of a detailed account of the story, lasting around two sentences. Interview extracts, called **clips**, are edited down and the reporter writes links which are a couple of lines leading into the next piece of actuality. This is followed by the reporter's voice either summing up or introducing another piece of actuality. The wrap ends with the station's standard out-cue, or **SOC**, such as 'Freda Smith, Radio Anytown News'.

This is how the wrap for this story might go ... **in** denotes the opening words on the cart and **out** the last statement so the presenter is warned when they need to start speaking again. **Dur** indicates the length of the cart.

An inquiry's been launched into what caused the Manchester motorway bridge disaster. All the bodies have now been recovered ... twenty-seven people have died.

Steve Solo reports.

As the emergency services clear away the wreckage people are already asking how could it happen?

The officer leading the disaster operation Superintendent Jim Bourne says it's too soon to say ...

IN: At this stage ...
OUT: ... information later.
DUR: 079

But construction expert Dr Tracey Sullivan believes close attention must focus on the controversial techniques used to build the bridge over Fulwood Brook ...

IN: We warned them ...
OUT: ... be avoided.
DUR: 08'

The Health and Safety Executive inquiry's expected to last at least six months.

Steve Solo – Manchester News.

As well as supplying his own station with from-the-scene reports, Steve will also find himself in considerable demand from a national newsroom. If he works in the commercial sector, IRN will want a report to feed to the rest of the network of independent stations. The same principle works for the BBC. He'll be expected to update with fresh voicers and wraps as events unfold, interview survivors, attend press conferences

> held by emergency services and generally be in two places at once gathering as much material as possible. The scene of such a disaster would be saturated with reporters, and competition to talk to witnesses and relatives in such a situation is intense.

Feeding that material to a national newsroom involves using the radio car to transmit the report from the car back to your station, which in turn passes it on to the national newsroom.The race to file fuels sheer exhilaration, particularly when a rival is roundly beaten.

THE STRUCTURE OF THE RADIO NEWSROOM

Job descriptions and titles vary according to whether a post is at a BBC or independent radio station. BBC journalists usually have to fill more airtime and tend to be jacks-of-all-trades. They must be able to fulfil many roles, from reporting to reading to editing to producing for a range of different types of programme. On the other hand, those working in commercial radio base their activities around preparing stories for hourly bulletins which usually last no more than four minutes.

(a) Commercial Local Radio (ILR)

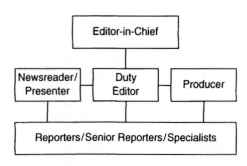

(b) BBC Local Radio

Radio journalism: job descriptions

The following positions are found in most newsrooms.

News editor
The news editor has overall editorial and managerial control of the station's news and current affairs output and is responsible to the station's management. Like newspaper editors their role is partly managerial and partly journalistic although the proportion of time spent on each will depend upon the individual station.

On the managerial side, they have to manage news staff and a budget for news production. They also have to oversee the news-making process on a practical level, ensuring good liaison with external sources of news and national outlets such as the BBC network or Independent Radio News.

These are individuals with considerable experience as journalists and broadcasters and tend to have worked their way to the top of the ladder. They are enthusiastic journalists who play a leading role in the newsroom operation and may read bulletins and report on major news stories. They give the final word on stories and are called upon to advise on the legality or suitability of a package. Therefore they must have rock-solid judgment and will often be called upon to defend their decisions when under attack. Radio teams work under tremendous pressure and news editors must have good leadership qualities and excellent communication skills to coordinate the activities of the newsroom.

Case study: Head of News and Sport, large commercial radio station

After gaining a postgraduate NCTJ certificate and indentures with the *East Anglian Daily Times* in Ipswich, our case study worked for BBC Local Radio, BBC Radio Wales then the Today programme on BBC Radio 4. He then moved to Radio Clyde, a commercial station in Glasgow: 'I hadn't tried ILR and liked what they were doing. It was important to get a broad base.' He moved stations 11 years ago as news editor and was promoted to head of news five years ago.

This is his day:

I wake up and listen to the 7am news bulletin on my station

and on other stations. If I have any queries about the news bulletin we are doing I will 'phone up and ask why we are doing it – in the nicest possible way. This does not happen very often because we have a very experienced staff in the newsroom and they can probably do it better than I can.

He arrives at the station between 8.30 and 9am to start his 10-hour working day in time for the news conference with the duty news editor. They discuss which stories are to be covered in what order and which reporters to allocate to them. If a story needs to be covered outside the office, they consider whether to send the reporter with the radio car. If any stories are already prepared for, such as the outcome of a court case for which the team have already completed background pieces, the news editor and duty news editor will work out how they can be incorporated into coverage of the verdict. This meeting is usually fairly short, about 15 minutes.

The rest of day is a mixture of administration, such as looking after the newsroom budget. The news editor is now part of the management team but, as much as possible, will sit on the newsdesk and assist the duty editor by acting as a reporter chasing up stories and by offering guidance if needed.

While the news editor has overall control of the newsroom, the duty news editor is in charge of intake and output during their own shift.

Duty editor

The duty editor is a senior journalist who is assigned to run the newsdesk, which is the hub of the newsmaking process, for a shift. They are on the frontline for receiving all the calls from potential news sources such as the public, emergency services and politicians. These stories are judged on merit and either passed on to a reporter, or fobbed off. The duty editor decides, after consultation with the news editor, what should be broadcast and in what order, which stories to include and which to omit. Their working day/night begins with the hand-over. This is when the retiring duty editor briefs them on what has been covered already, how many times the story has been broadcast already, and what reporters are currently working on. The duty editor then checks incoming stories from staff, freelances and agencies and briefs reporters on new stories.

The duty editor regularly checks with the emergency services to see if any crimes, fires or accidents worthy of coverage are occurring. At the same time, they will be keeping an ear open to rival stations to check they are not missing any important stories or angles. The duty editor often reads the news so they will amend or rewrite reporters' copy to suit their reading style. After a programme, they will log which stories have been read, in what order and how many times they have been read that day so they can check at a glance whether there has been too much repetition. As a senior journalist, the duty editor may also report and write stories where required but they never leave the office while on duty.

The role demands careful team-playing because, the following week, the duty editor might be working as a reporter for one of their colleagues who has been rostered to replace them on the newsdesk. So the duty editor needs to delegate tasks calmly and should offer constructive criticism, not insults, to the reporter who forgets to load their recorder with tape. Journalistically, the duty editor is in charge of the newsroom so they must have the skills and confidence to judge the best running order and guide reporters to the best angles. They should also be willing to refer up to their news editor for guidance when in doubt. It can take several years to reach duty editor level in the BBC while in commercial stations, where staffing numbers are lower, a new member of staff might be put in charge of the newsdesk during a late night shift very quickly.

News producer
This post is virtually extinct in music-based commercial radio. In the BBC, both at local and national level, the producer has a key role in speech-based programme-making. It is similar to that of the duty editor in that the producer decides how a subject is approached. The position is different in that it's focused specifically on one show, for example breakfast or evening drive-time programmes. The producer advises reporters on how to approach a story, for example whether adding music is appropriate. He or she will also line up live guests for the show. The producer has overall responsibility for what goes where in a programme to create an overall tone, mixing heavyweight news stories with lighter items.

The job can be fast and furious because news can break at the most awkward of times. This means a producer often makes decisions while the programme is going out on air. As well as

guiding reporters in what is required of them, the producer may
well also be called upon to create special documentaries on a particular topic. They use their expertise in production techniques to
mix sound and script with music and archive material to achieve
the most attention-grabbing effect.

Reporters and senior reporters
Reporters who are relatively new to the medium vary in their allocated duties and responsibilities according to the station they work
for. For example, BBC recruits may have to shadow experienced
staff for some time before being given free reign to cover a story on
their own. Elsewhere, reporters are placed in charge of the news
desk for an hour or two to develop confidence and news judgment. Generally, they are required to originate ideas for stories and
prepare material for broadcast as well as respond to assignments
they are handed by the duty news editor. Their role includes
research, finding appropriate spokespeople, writing cues and
briefing the duty editor as they follow the story's development
during the day. Reporters are expected to edit tape for broadcast
and undertake simple reporting and interviews. Writing scripts
and finding and editing illustrative audio are additional duties.

A commitment to news and current affairs coupled with dedication, energy and a good broadcast voice are vital qualities in a
reporter. Radio reporters sometimes enter the medium with no
previous radio experience but often after working in print.
Whatever their background, they must be able to demonstrate a
keen awareness of radio in terms of its treatment of stories.

Senior reporters are experienced journalists who are required
not only to report but also to produce, duty edit and present.
They bring greater depth and expertise to stories they work on
and, where the station permits it, work on longer programmes
and documentaries determining the shape and content of what is
broadcast. A great deal of editorial judgment is required as senior
journalists have to originate and develop ideas and react to
stories as they break. That often means directing other staff and
commissioning work from outside journalists. They often duty
edit a programme, which means overseeing newsgathering and
output on a shift basis. Many senior journalists, especially in the
BBC, are expected to have an informed knowledge of a specific
area, such as social affairs, education, health, law, business or the
environment. Not all senior journalists have radio experience,

but they should have substantial experience in print plus an understanding and commitment to broadcasting.

Case study: Reporter who has worked in both BBC and independent sector

After graduating in Combined Arts, this journalist gained a place on the Postgraduate Diploma Course in Journalism Studies at University College, Cardiff. He worked first with BBC Radio Lincolnshire then moved to BBC Radio Bedfordshire where he stayed four years. When Radio City in Liverpool started a second, all-talk station, he moved into the commercial sector, staying as senior journalist for four years before going into national radio journalism with Independent Radio News in London. He was attracted to the profession early, acting as village reporter for a freesheet while still at school, helping produce a student newspaper at Poly and working for a youth radio show during the summer holidays.

The reasons for my interest then still stand. If you're interested in what goes on around you why there's no better job to go for. Plus, no day's the same and you never know who you'll be meeting or in what situation. The buzz when a hot story's breaking is thrillingly intense so once you're hooked it's difficult to kick.

He says he believes the role of the media in a democratic society is a vital one and not to be taken lightly: 'I relish challenging authority, making people justify their actions. Being paid to ask awkward questions of people in positions of authority is a privilege and luxury and not to be taken lightly.'

To succeed in radio journalism, the practitioner needs stamina, accuracy and dedication just like in any medium. 'You'll need to be able to write quickly,' he adds.

If a story drops just minutes before the bulletin (another name for programme) it must get on air. Technical brilliance is not vital. Picking up how to use a recorder and studio comes quickly to most, though the finer points do take longer to master. A strong, clear voice is essential, though accent is less important.

Our journalist says the high points of his job are many, especially the autonomy and control he has over his work. In addition, 'When a story of national importance occurs all hell breaks loose. Order has to be made from chaos and the satisfaction of operating despite the pressure is considerable ... particularly when your voice gets onto broadcasts across the country.' The low points include unpaid overtime and inevitable routine. 'When nothing's happened it's a considerable chore calling the emergency services every hour to find exactly nothing has moved. But you never know what might be around the corner ... and that's the secret of what keeps every journalist going.'

Specialists

These tend to be good all-round senior journalists who can demonstrate considerable expertise in a particular field such as science and technology, health, entertainment and the arts. It's not enough to be enthusiastic about the area, specialist reporters have to have good contacts within their field and be able to break the stories before their competitors. To command such authority, it is usually essential to have a degree or other qualification in a relevant subject. Specialists are also sometimes called upon to react spontaneously to a development within their area on air. That means they must be able to speak about their subject clearly and precisely and in a way that can be understood by the non-specialist listener. To reach the position of specialist reporter, journalists will usually have worked extensively at reporter and senior reporter level. This demonstrates to the news editor that they have the expertise and judgment to work independently. The specialist will have already shown a good track record generating stories relevant to their field. Alternatively, the station may simply designate a member of staff to be the local government reporter or business correspondent and they will be required to acquaint themselves with the subject.

Bi-media journalist

For many years, radio and television have been separate entities under a wide diversity of management styles. In 1987, the BBC created a News and Current Affairs Directorate to enable network radio and television journalists to work together under clear guidelines and similar management structures. This bi-media policy also exists on a regional level and within ITN radio and television.

Some critics say that bi-media working has reduced standards by expecting radio journalists, who are used to working with sound, to be able to adapt their skills to work with pictures.

The Head of IRN explains for us the process and ideology behind bi-media reporting. He says that while radio and television reporting are very separate skills with different production values, there is an overlap on both sides; for example, reporting from Westminster on things going on in the House of Commons, is an area where there is a good deal of overlap. TV is dominated by pictures but there aren't a lot of pictures in political reporting other than the Chamber itself and shots of faces, and stories tend to be fairly straightforward. He says:

> Radio reporters at Westminster have carried out a large number of interviews for TV using camera crews. Likewise television reporters have also done straightforward voice reports for radio. TV reporters in the field, say Rwanda or Bosnia, will file radio reports for us and again we have helped TV by providing 'phone interviews when they haven't got time to provide moving pictures. It's a sort of evolutionary process, a coming together of skills.

IRN reporters receive a work placement on the television side because ITN believes it better use of everyone's time if everyone in the company has at least an understanding of how television news is constructed. He concludes: 'The vast bulk of the revenue we earn is from television so everyone here should at least have a grasp of television.'

NEW AND FUTURE DEVELOPMENTS IN RADIO JOURNALISM

Radio is re-assessing its relationship with its audience and meeting listeners' more sophisticated expectations of the medium by harnessing and developing computer technology. Technology is also solving problems journalists didn't realize they had. Radio newsrooms are traditionally equipped with machines using quarter-inch tape which has to be physically cut with a razor blade, and edited by sticking it together with tape and that is after transferring audio from cassettes onto tape reels. Individual

news reports are broadcast from re-usable carts physically fed
into a console by the bulletin reader. A medium relying on both
speed and sound obviously has to ensure it is of the best possible
quality which has prompted a host of technical innovations
which are transforming radio news and current affairs production. No longer do journalists have to wade ankle deep in a
spaghetti-like mess of brown tape or guesstimate the length of
cues. Now it's all done digitally.

The Chief Engineer at IRN keeps up to date with some of the
most recent broadcasting innovations. The main changes in that
organization, which is a service transmitting hourly news bulletins and stories to independent radio stations nationwide, have
occurred in the last two years during which time journalists have
used traditional quarter-inch tape machines. If staff wanted to
receive audio items from one of the independent stations for
transmission throughout the network, it involved a fairly
complicated procedure of setting up a fixed, one-to-one circuit
called a landline from the station into the IRN newsroom which
could cost in the region of £7000 a year to rent. As an alternative,
they had a system with breakpoints part way down the country
where they could switch routes which was again costly to run.

ISDN, Integrated Services Digital Network, had been around
for a long time and is a system for transporting computer data.
Broadcaster manufacturers started to hit upon using it for audio
transferral in 1992 because it enables quality audio to be transferred down a telephone line. As with computer data, the system
transforms the information to be carried into a digital series of
bleeps which can be transported down the line. Receivers at
the destination unscramble the message back into sounds.
ISDN means easier maintenance and the same dial-up charges as
ordinary telephone calls with a higher standard charge per
quarter. There are one or two drawbacks: with computers, if
there is an error in transmitting the message, it will indicate that
and the missing data will automatically be retransferred.

This cannot be done with audio because you would get
repeated words which would not make sense. There are also
limitations to where you can put an ISDN point; it has to be close
to a telephone exchange or it won't work, as IRN discovered
when they tried to use ISDN lines to transmit audio from a
water-skiing championship in Reading. Telephone engineers
tried to cut down the distance from the exchange and the hotel

which was the press centre by running the cable across the water-skiing lake. They had the engineer sat on the back of the boat with a reel of cable as the water-skier was ploughing across the water.

It is the innovations possible with ISDN which could have impact on journalists' work. While ISDN can currently only connect one person to another person like a traditional telephone call, broadcasters are talking to the operators of 0891-style services to see if 'story banks' could be set up. Journalists working for or subscribing to, say, IRN's services could dial into the computerized bank using an ISDN line and either deposit a news story or record one stored there for transmission. Journalists would pull up a story menu on their VDU, dial a number on a telephone in the studio and record the audio ready for broadcast on their own programme. An added possibility introduced by ISDN is that stations could broadcast live audio, not just pre-recorded as is the case at present. Currently, if a reporter is filing from location to the studio, a colleague has to receive their call in a recording booth and physically record the audio. Instead, the reporter could dial straight into the newsroom computer. Stations subscribing to the service could be charged in the same way as 0891-type callers.

Computer disks, either floppies or CDs, are taking over from traditional bulky tape cartridges for storing and playing reports. Whereas magnetic tape was sometimes unreliable and the machinery's moving parts needed maintenance, computer drives have less moving parts and can be upgraded cheaply and connected up together. The benefits to the journalist editing digitally on computer disk is that mistakes can easily be patched up. Even the most experienced quarter-inch tape editor can accidentally razor off the last syllable of a word. Repairing the damage means hunting around on the floor for the missing inch of tape! Digitally, you mark start and stop points on the computer screen and just listen to it. The raw material remains intact and can be re-edited by someone else if needed.

Tape recorders used by reporters are likely to be replaced by mini-computers. The size of an A5 pad, the new recorders will have a plug in microphone but the similarity ends there as there are no moving parts and audio is recorded on a 2 × 2.5 inch digital card. The machine has an editing facility with an LCD display plus built in ISDN-linking facilities. The main obstacle to local radio is cost, now approximately £10 000 for one machine, but prices should eventually come down.

At the BBC, it was the development of satellite technology that made World Service Television possible. Satellite has also transformed the quality of much of World Service Radio's output. And another technological revolution is on the cards: Digital Audio Broadcasting (DAB). DAB will work by radio receivers picking up digital signals direct from satellites. Experts say sound quality will be almost as good as compact disks. With the first tests of DAB taking place in Britain in 1994, the BBC says a global network of three or four satellites would deliver excellent reception in even the remotest parts of the world.

While technology is transforming radio production and transmission, the organization of radio is also undergoing change, moving more into niche broadcasting. As the Government releases more and more wavelengths to bidders, areas which are currently served by two or three stations may in the not-too-distant future have ten services. They cannot all expect to attract mass audiences and so stations devoted to news or jazz or drama may be established with a clear identity of their own. A 24-hour rolling local news station would inevitably compete with news coverage on exiting established stations. The BBC might think very carefully about whether it wants to invest a lot of money in its reporting strength and an established commercial station might consider whether it really needs to have as much news and information and concentrate on music. 'News will always be preserved because there is a great thirst for it but the things that might change are length and the amount that you do,' says the Head of News and Sport at Liverpool's Radio City.

So it would seem that the future for those entering the medium now will rely on them being adaptable and multi-skilled to make the most of the challenges ahead. Far from being a blind medium, radio is forever on the look-out for innovative opportunities to ensure its success when set against the burgeoning competition from print and television. As most of us will testify, life without radio, as we butter our toast, sit in the bath or drive our car, would be very dull indeed. It looks set to offer a rewarding career to journalists for a long time yet.

6

Television

'Good evening, and welcome to the news ...' For so many aspiring journalists, the ultimate pinnacle of their careers is the chance to sit in front of a camera and deliver those words to the nation. But you would be mistaken for thinking working in television means automatically seeing your face on the screen. In broadcasting, the term 'journalist' applies to many different grades of staff and the vast majority of television journalists are embroiled in the busy and rewarding backroom world of reporting and production.

With around 2000 full-time journalists working in the sector, television is a small industry yet it plays such a dramatic role in our lives. Without even realizing it, we can be greatly influenced by television over everything from our views about the world to our taste in music. Those who work in television are quick to confess it is not as glamorous as people might believe but there can be little doubt that the TV journalist's pulse is racing that much faster than their print colleague's as their deadline looms.

How is television journalism different
from any other type of journalism?

Television journalism involves dual skills in that the practitioner has to be a capable, concise writer and they must also mediate news in a visual way. You have to develop a visual highlight of a story in a way that will enhance and illustrate the spoken word. Television by its very nature has to entertain. That does not mean reporting has to be humorous or flippant but it should capture the imagination and leave the viewer feeling informed and stimulated, not bored or distracted. Because of the time pressures, television news has to say a lot with very few words and pictures. A news package on a television programme may last just three minutes and comprise a total of only 100 words. That is very little when compared with a story in a newspaper which may be 500 words long, giving the print journalist more scope for detail and analysis. By contrast, an hour-long documentary involves a tremendous amount of time and preparation to convey the material in an interesting way with words and pictures. Unlike print journalism, it is a highly technical process involving the skills of dozens of people. In other ways, the news-gathering process in television is the same as in any other medium. Journalists have to keep on top of everyday issues and events as well as maintain good contacts and deal with the unexpected. Because of limited airtime, less words may be used than in print journalism and the pictures will often speak for themselves. The story-count is lower than in newspapers so news editors have to be far more ruthless in selecting the biggest and best stories of the day for coverage and transmission.

There is a great deal of forward-planning in television. All important dates, such as political conferences, elections, sporting events and so on are prepared far ahead. Some criticize this as being news management but there are logistical reasons why coverage often has to be predicted months in advance; for example, provision may have to be made for special facilities on location to feed footage back to the studio, and extra staff may have to be brought in and background research may be needed. Television journalists have to interpret, not just present the news, so innovation, flair and creativity are part of the TV journalist's job.

What is the work of a television journalist like?

The prestige and financial rewards associated with television journalism still make it a magnet for would-be journalists and for those already working in the industry. It needs no stressing, however, that if getting onto a local paper is challenging when there are thousands of titles in existence, landing a TV job is even harder. There are few vacancies available and those that are tend to be filled internally. It takes a very dynamic – and lucky – individual to walk straight into a TV news post. All will tell you that the work is highly-pressured. News programmes go out live and the material has to be as up-to-date as possible which means there is little or no time to prepare or rehearse. Timing of packages and the presenters' scripts has to be immaculate as an item cannot over-run by a few seconds without disrupting the whole programme or bulletin.

Harnessing the two dimensions of pictures and sound can be a very persuasive and powerful way of communicating news. But it can also be terribly frustrating as getting a story from its conception to the screen can be a rather long, drawn-out process, especially in the case of documentaries which are often only finished minutes before broadcast to ensure they are right up to date. Once a print journalist has gathered their interviews, it is a case of just writing the words. For a television journalist that is just the start as they must also obtain on-screen interviews, library footage and background music where necessary, book time in an editing suite and ensure all the required technical aspects are catered for.

Modern technological innovation has transformed the tele-vision newsmaking process: computer graphics have replaced artist's impressions, videotape has replaced film and news is gathered and produced electronically using satellites and the latest computerized facilities. This has not only had the effect of making the process more immediate – journalists can create packages that contain the very latest information – it has also globalized TV news to the extent that anything happening in any part of the world can now be brought to our screens as it happens. The standards are higher, the job is faster and more pressured and only the best can survive in a career that demands instant news judgment, instant creativity and, hardest of all, instant energy.

The future for anyone managing to break into television is positive with many options open to a flexible worker. Once you have gained initial off-screen experience, you can work your way into producing, editing or on-screen presenting. There are also opportunities in the technical and managerial sides. The main choice comes when you see the scope for different types of programme involvement. You could work for a nightly news programme with its instant and spontaneous fast-moving output then transfer to a documentary series which would enable you to exercise more creativity and develop your production skills.

As the periodical industry is expanding to encompass the increasing number of titles on offer, made possible by cheaper publishing costs, broadcasting is experiencing growth both in terms of the number of services available to viewers and listeners and the independent production firms set up to supply programmes to them. Advances in cable and satellite technology and the introduction of 24-hour rolling television dictates that there are likely to be more opportunities opening up for journalists within the medium. However, the trend appears to be to restrict the number of staff jobs but increase intake of freelance and short-contract workers which means the profession can be unstable and lacking in security. However, many people are happy working on a freelance basis as it gives them the flexibility and freedom to move around and gain wide experience.

THE SHAPE OF THE TELEVISION INDUSTRY

Nationally, television broadcasting comes from the public-sector British Broadcasting Corporation (BBC) and the independent, commercial sector. The BBC is divided into six regions with three in England (North, Midlands and East and South) and one each for Scotland, Ireland and Wales. Regional centres have their own specialities, such as youth productions, as much network programming has been decentralized from London to the regions.

All the regional TV stations have their own newsrooms which liaise closely with BBC News and Current Affairs at Broadcasting House and Television Centre, both of which are based in central London. Journalists in the regions produce material for local programmes and their packages may also be submitted for network broadcast if the story is of nationwide relevance.

Nationally, the BBC broadcasts several flagship news programmes each day as well as documentaries and investigative programmes. The BBC's regional daily news programmes have a different agenda from those of the ITV companies. The BBC will report big issues of national significance and apply a regional angle to them which tends to give the programme a very authoritative tone. Often a full 30-minute slot will be devoted to one topic. The BBC recently moved well-known national newsreaders to the regions to anchor the regional news programmes with the aim of heightening their authority to the same level as that of national news.

Conversely, ITV regional news programmes are keen to take their viewers on a journey from one part of the area to another to show that they are very much part of the community in which their audience resides. Reporters have districts to cover and programmes will attempt to include items from most districts to achieve balance and a familiar rapport with the audience.

At the end of the day, content of BBC and ITV news programmes is similar because they operate under the same news values. The lead story might be the same for both programmes when a major incident has taken place. However, on a quieter news day there may be greater diversity. Viewing figures would suggest that viewers accept both the BBC and ITV formats.

The independent sector consists of Channel Three covering the regional independent companies' ITV network, Channel Four and the proposed Channel Five. There are also countless satellite and cable channels.

There are 16 independent companies presently holding 10-year-long ITV franchises. Some of these produce and broadcast their own programmes as well as supplying to the network as a whole which is run centrally by ITV Network Centre. Other franchise holders act as publisher broadcasters and take all of their input from independent production companies. They may, in turn, submit these programmes to Network Centre for consideration for national network transmission.

News and current affairs output by the independent sector usually comes from regional newsrooms and from Independent Television News (ITN) which at the time of writing has an exclusive contract with the ITV companies to supply national and international news.

Channel Four first went on air in 1982 as a result of the 1981 Broadcasting Act. Its news is also supplied by ITN and many current affairs programmes are bought-in as Channel Four is a publisher, not a maker, of programmes. S4C is the fourth channel in Wales set up to provide a Welsh language service for approximately 35 hours a week and to broadcast Channel Four's output the rest of the time.

Sky Television was launched by News International in February 1989 as a four-channel service including Europe's first 24-hour news channel and Britain's first subscription TV network. In November 1990, British Satellite Broadcasting (BSB) merged with Sky to create British Sky Broadcasting which currently offers six channels including news. More than three million homes are presently connected to the networks by satellite or by cable.

All UK broadcasters are state-regulated to a degree. The BBC is authorized to be self-regulating under the Royal Charter while all other TV broadcasters are monitored by the Independent Television Commission (ITC) under the authority of the 1990 Broadcasting Act. In this Act, the face of British television broadcasting was transformed by the introduction of a free-market approach to what had until then been a duopoly of the BBC and ITV. On screen, the innovations in satellite and cable technology, coupled with the new legislation, mean we can tap into countless English-language channels and some foreign. Off-screen, the industry is expanding to create more work opportunities in this exciting medium.

Now that you have the framework of this dynamic, exciting and expanding medium, let us focus upon the work that television journalists do to transform an idea for a story into a report, and then how that report is incorporated into a whole programme. Television stations are all unique so what follows can only be a guide to typical practices. Why not try to spend some time at a local station to find out what they do?

Television reporting

Once a television journalist has got a great idea for a story, there is a lot of hard work to be done before that item goes on air. In this section we will look at the two main aspects of television's journalistic production – intake and output.

- **Intake** covers the newsgathering process. This is the collection and packaging of stories from a variety of sources including the station's own staff, agencies, freelance reporters and so on.

- **Output** covers the production and broadcast of programmes which involves putting the stories into a running order and incorporating other presentational material such as graphics.

The timescale of intake and output will vary according to the organization and the type of programme. For example, it might take less than two hours from start to finish in the case of a lunchtime news programme whereas a documentary may take months of research, filming and editing.

The following account will be based on production of a daily network news programme, starting with the way a story is packaged for television.

Gathering stories for television

There are news days and there are blues days whatever medium you are working in. Good stories do not fall into journalists' laps in television any more than in print or radio. It takes hard work. Armed with a thick contacts book, the TV reporter must keep the newsdesk stocked with sufficient material to fill at least one daily programme, and the stories need to look as good as they sound. Pictures are vital to a good television report otherwise the audience would just switch off.

The station's editorial team hold their morning news conference at 8.30am to discuss the prospects for that evening's 7pm 30-minute programme. The news editor, who is in charge of intake, that is getting the news in, allocates stories to reporters and crews, which usually consist of a camera operator and occasionally a sound recordist if, for example, the report is to be filmed in high winds where special equipment and expertise would be needed. If lighting conditions are poor, a lighting person will be dispatched with the crew.

The story can be covered on location or by bringing guests into the studio for questioning. Once the journalist has acquainted themselves with the facts of the story, which might be done by telephone interviews and reading about the subject, the reporter then has to assess the situation and decide on the best way to present the story.

A television interview normally starts before the cameras roll with what is called a pre-chat. This is where the reporter briefs the interviewee on the kind of questions they will be asking and also puts inexperienced spokespeople at ease. While this is going on, the lighting will be rigged up and the sound recordist will 'mic up' both reporter and interviewee and test levels. Interviewees are asked to put their points across directly and concisely so as to get the maximum amount of detail across in the least amount of time. A completed package might last a minute and a half which means there is no time for long, intricate answers. Notwithstanding, the journalist will ask open-ended questions, as discussed in Chapter 1, which elicit more than 'yes' or 'no' answers.

During the interview, the camera operator will shoot the conversation, focusing mainly on head-and-shoulder views of the interviewee. There are two main types of camera used in television broadcasting, film cameras and electronic cameras which use videotape. News programmes tend to use electronic cameras, known as electronic news gathering (ENG) equipment because videotape (VT) is quicker and easier to edit – essential for fast broadcasting.

Once the interview is complete and the spokesperson thanked, the reporter talks directly to the camera giving the audience background information to the issue or event (piece-to-camera). Stories filmed in this way tend to be done out of sequence so it is important that the reporter can brief the VT (video-tape) editor as to the correct order the footage should take for viewing.

In the final stage the camera operator points the camera at the reporter who will repeat the questions as they were asked to the interviewee plus nod (noddies) and respond as if in reaction to what the interviewee said. These questions and reactions are then edited into the piece to add visual interest but also to avoid jump-cuts. This happens when part of what the interviewee says is edited out causing the picture to jump unnaturally.

If the report has been shot close to transmission outside the studio, the crew may be armed with a portable editing suite which enables them quickly to edit the interview and transmit it back to the studio electronically. If there is more time, the reporter will return to base and go into an editing booth with a VT editor and work on the material with them. In smaller set-ups, the camera person or reporter might edit the package themselves.

Editing the piece

The programme producer, who is in charge of the way the broadcast will go out, gives the team an exact length in minutes and seconds for their report. Timing has to be meticulous or the whole programme might under- or overrun which has major repercussions for scheduling (and advertising). The editing booth contains videotape players, monitors and mixing hardware. A time code, counting the number of hours, minutes, seconds and frames appears on screen as the tape is played. This is a guide to the editing sequence:

1. The 'rushes' as the unedited tape is called, is logged so the team can trace exactly where each section can be found on the tape.
2. The reporter and editor examine their material and decide which sections to use and in what order.
3. The editor types in the start and finish time of the section of tape they wish to digitally cut and paste to the master tape which is the cassette bearing the finished report. The machine then copies, or dubs as it is called, that section over at the press of a button without altering the original recording. This is far quicker and simpler than film which has to be developed and physically cut, meaning it can only be used once and damage is irreparable.

   The package will usually begin with scene-setting shots or archive footage to act as an introduction to the piece. This will be accompanied by a verbal introduction by the reporter superimposed over the pictures leading to the interview or interviews which help to explain all sides of the story. The interviews will be interspersed with one or two paragraphs of further expansion by the reporter accompanied by relevant and interesting images or even graphics. The final shot will act as a conclusion to the package.
4. Once visual elements of the story are edited together, the reporter types their story onto a typewriter or more commonly a VDU screen. Sometimes, the reporter writes their script before editing so that the pictures are cut to fit the script. The report begins with a **cue** which is a paragraph preparing the viewer for what is to come. This is accompanied by an establishing shot, such as the camera panning, or sweeping over, a view of a piece of countryside threatened by a new motorway. The reporter takes care to allow the pictures to speak for themselves and avoids using unnecessary words or statements describing what viewers can see for themselves on screen. The copy is written in the form of a script which carries **in words** and **out words** to tell the director in the gallery when the report is starting and finishing. The out words are commonly standard style for the

station, such as 'Freda Bloggs for News at Nine at Westminster'. This is known as a standard out cue or SOC. They then go into a booth and record the report over the relevant sections of footage, the duration of which is marked on their script. A sound recordist mixes the reporter's voice with any sound on the tape so that background noise fades as the journalist talks. The voicer, as it is called, may be recorded several times at different speeds to fit in with the editing.

5. The final step is to provide what is called a headline, a piece of footage lasting only a few seconds to be shown at the very start of the programme when the presenter introduces the contents. This is only done if requested by the producer.

Here is an extract from a script for a prerecorded television news report where a reporter has written their story to fit the edited footage. TV scripts must give details of graphics and footage and their durations. Cues represent the number of seconds or minutes from the start of the report that the reporter should read that part of the script. Note there is a two-second gap left at the beginning so the reporter's voice does not clash with the newsreader's.

N/READER	Ten people have been injured in scuffles following tonight's FA Cup semi-final match. Kate Ward has this report:
CUE 02″	This was the scene on the streets of London shortly after Monktown City's two-nil victory over Dunford United.
CUE 11″	Local residents described what they saw.
Residents IN: 'I heard a ...' OUT: '... it ever before' 25″	
CUE 27″	The injured, who received mostly cuts and grazes, were ferried by ambulance to ...

Knowing all the technical ingredients for constructing a tele-vision report is one thing; to capture the interest of the viewer when combining words with pictures is quite another, requiring flair and imagination. A former Head of Journalism Training at the BBC said: 'A good way to tell whether someone is producing a good television report is to close your eyes and listen to the words. If they are doing it properly, you should want to see what's on the screen. Without pictures there should be something missing.'

It is frequently the case where there are several news programmes within which the report might be broadcast that the journalist is required to produce the package in a few different formats to avoid repetition.

At this stage, intake of that story is complete and the tape is cued up for transmission. Meanwhile, the producer is working on the output, preparing the programme for broadcast.

Producing the programme

The programme producer is responsible for co-ordinating the efforts of journalists, editors, graphic artists and others to ensure all the right material is prepared correctly in time for transmis-sion. The producer holds updating meetings with programme personnel including editors, reporters and graphic artists throughout the day to hammer out the correct running order. On most days, the lead story is so big it is obviously going to be the main headline. On other days, there may be so many good – or bad – stories to choose from that a great deal of discussion must take place. At these meetings, the producer hammers out the way stories should be angled, that is what the top line of the piece should be, and whether the story should be accompanied by graphics, live reports such as via satellite links to sporting events overseas. These meetings are also an opportunity for any member of the journalistic team to give their input on how the programme might be shaped and everyone leaves in no doubt as to what they must do. For example, a journalist might be sent away to re-edit their package to a different length or to include an extra spokesperson.

Meanwhile, presenters read through their scripts which have been written by reporters, researchers and producers, and make any amendments where they feel necessary. The vast majority of television news presenters are seasoned journalists. They will have attended all the day's news conferences and will have discussed how they might approach a live interview, for instance.

As broadcast time looms, late reports will still be coming in and the running order of the programme might be updated at any time should a big story break or a dynamic new twist to a running topic come to light. A brief rehearsal takes place about 30 minutes before going on air. This is the responsibility of the director who has the task of blending the camera shots, co-ordinating the graphics with the reports and ensuring the programme sticks to its strict timing.

Going on air

The pristine presenters are sat at their consoles, their earpieces picking up every single word that is uttered in the gallery which is the control centre of the programme's broadcast. Meanwhile, some of the tape reports are still being edited and have not yet reached the gallery with only seconds to go before transmission! This probably means that the presenter has not received their script yet either, but they do not bat an eyelid. As countdown begins, the atmosphere is tense and, to the untrained eye, chaotic. The gallery is a room packed with monitors which record the perspective of each of the studio cameras and allow the tape players to cue up each cart, the format each taped report and section of graphics is stored on.

During each item, the gallery team (consisting of director, production assistant (PA), vision mixer who cuts or fades from one shot to another, grams operator who plays the signature tune and any other sound effects and the lighting director) watch the monitors and call out which captions, graphics and reports should go on air at precisely what moment. Meanwhile, the presenter coolly performs a live studio interview regardless of the aural onslaught going on down their earpiece.

As the credits roll at the end of the broadcast, calm is restored and the team thank one another for yet another smooth performance. For the director and their team, it's all in a day's work.

Not all programmes are assembled in this way. With advances in technology to harness ENG and demands from the audience for real-time 'live' coverage, TV stations, particularly those devoted to rolling news, are making greater use of the outside broadcast.

The outside broadcast

The OB, as it is known in the business, once struck a note of horror in the heart of producers before the days of videotape as it required intense planning, scores of personnel and vast amounts of expensive hardware. Today, a two-person crew can transmit live pictures to our screens from anywhere in the world. For major events such as the cup final or a royal wedding, the full scale OB unit is launched into action. In simple terms, an OB is a mobile television station that allows almost anything that can be done in an indoor TV studio to be done on location. The unit consists of a large van which operates as the control room. With its array of monitors and switches, it resembles the gallery in the studio and houses the director, producer and engineers and the team keep in touch with camera operators and reporters via radio earpieces. Reports and pictures are relayed via cable or microwave to the station's master control room for broadcast.

Now we have a picture of how television news is put together, we will take a closer look at who the key people are who make it happen.

THE STRUCTURE OF THE TELEVISION NEWSROOM

To the viewer, television news and current affairs looks slick, professional and glamorous so it may come as a surprise to learn that the picture behind-the-scenes is hectic and pressured. Fictional depictions of television present it quite differently but there is no room for egos or anyone not prepared to work hard and be flexible.

It is important to stress that it is very difficult to start out as a television journalist. While some traineeships exist they are rare and most television recruits are already senior journalists with several years' experience in print and/or radio.

Television journalism: job descriptions

Here is a description of the main journalistic roles you would encounter in TV journalism; however every newsroom is different in terms of number of staff and their roles so it is only a guide. Not all the jobs listed will exist in every newsroom and many of the roles are not clear-cut. Journalists working on longer programmes and documentaries operate in small teams distinct from the personnel in the newsroom. These teams consist of researchers, reporters, a producer and a director and they will call upon the services of technical staff when required.

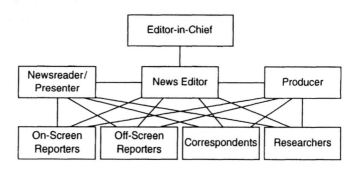

Editor-in-chief/news editor

Overall management and output of a specific programme or news service is organized by the editor-in-chief or news editor. This person undertakes the resource and personnel management essential to the efficient production of the department including negotiating budgets and recruitment of staff. They have a major journalistic role in deciding what to broadcast, in what order, which stories should be included and which are to be omitted. Much of their planning is done well ahead of their programme's deadline. At one television station, this person might influence both the content of a specific programme and the style in which it is presented. Alternatively the news editor might have overall control of several broadcasts, not just one programme. The following is a rundown of what their job involves.

1. They will be in charge of that day's news agenda which means they use their experience and judgment to select from the list of possible items exactly what is to be reported and to negotiate with the producer which stories will feature in the broadcast.

2. The running order and presentation style varies from programme to programme depending on available airtime and the type of audience who might be watching and the news editor is duty-bound to ensure coverage is suitable. For example, stories featuring violent footage must be carefully edited for early evening viewing when children might be watching only to be broadcast in full in a late night broadcast. The news editor is also a quality-controller who assesses whether the report is of a high-enough standard for broadcast in terms of content and appearance, and has the last word when it comes to factual accuracy and avoidance of reportage which might contravene libel or contempt of court laws. Television is additionally governed by strict rules concerning bias and political distortion for which the editor is publicly accountable.
3. Once the news editor has planned the content, they must ensure there are adequate reporters and crews allocated to cover all items.
4. As transmission time nears, the television newsroom becomes a highly charged environment and the news editor must ensure its smooth and efficient running up to the programme or bulletin.

An average working shift for an editor could be 15 hours so the person who takes on this role needs to have a great deal of energy and enthusiasm for what they do as well as the ability to keep their team motivated in a high-pressure environment. As this is one of the most senior editorial roles, the person would normally have considerable journalistic and broadcast experience. It is not unheard of for television news editors to be appointed straight from print media if they can demonstrate an understanding of the challenges of the medium, the effective mixing of words and pictures.

Programme producer
Producers are key players in making sure the news is broadcast in the best form to the audience. In other words, they are in charge of the **output** side of journalistic broadcasting, whereas the news editor deals with **input**. The role of producer varies according to the organization they work for. For example, rolling satellite news channels have large numbers of reporter/

producers who package stories using material from a variety of sources. In effect, their role is part reporting and part producing. A programme producer working for a network or regional news programme does not report, they have authority over the running order and presentation of that specific broadcast.

Whereas reporters and news editors gather and prepare the individual items, producers are responsible for how the whole programme is assembled. Producing requires liaising with many other staff and departments as you cannot do it alone. There are graphics to commission, music and other effects to obtain from the archives and it may be necessary to work closely with others on the script.

We looked earlier at the way a single programme might be produced for a network news programme. Let's now look at the work of a reporter/producer more closely and examine how their day might be organized when working for a 24-hour rolling cable news channel. This example is useful in showing how roles in television are becoming blurred.

8.00: Goes through the papers and the various agency wires including Reuters, Associated Press and the Press Association to acquaint themself generally with what is happening.

8.30: Attends the morning news conference which is addressed by the news editor who describes what stories are being covered throughout the day, who is covering them and what producers can expect from the reporters and when. This half-hour meeting is attended by the programme producer, section editors (business, foreign, etc.) and reporter/producers. After they finish going through their diary, the news editor says what has already been covered and what is cut from the previous evening, effectively news that's currently running.

Then for example the foreign news editor describes their prospects for the day in order for the producer to decide how they might deliver the story. For example, if the President of the USA was to deliver a speech on gun laws, the producer would need to make arrangements for a satellite link so the programme could drop in live during the speech. The foreign editor also describes what correspondents based abroad are covering and tells what is available on the foreign feeds provided by agencies covering the major flashpoints around the world. And the meeting will go on until all of the staff have input into the day's prospective coverage.

9.00: After the news conference follows the producers' meeting. The executive producer will state what s/he wants each producer to do. For example, one may be asked to produce a package on a foreign issue for noon using material obtained from agency feeds and writing it to suit the style of the programme. This is the reporting side of the reporter/producer's job and they might be expected to produce three packages in any one shift.

Noon: A producer working for this type of rolling channel will have many hours of television to fill and one of their chief roles is to select spokespeople to comment on current events and take part in live interviews and debates. They must use their journalistic authority and news awareness to select the right people, track them down through their extensive list of contacts then persuade them to take part.

15.00: If anything happens during the day internationally, the reporter/producer will approach the news editor to arrange telephone reports from the scene of the incident. If it's something domestic, the reporter/producer will start by obtaining telephone reports for live broadcast while at the same time inviting relevant spokespeople into the studio, by which time a colleague will already be working on a background package from library footage and the story gathers momentum. 'It's like a big rolling stone, the story gets bigger and bigger,' is how one reporter/producer describes the process.

17.00: A major part of the reporter/producer's job is to write links which are three or four paragraph introductions to the story for the presenter to read out on air. In addition, certain stories may need some explanation with graphics such as maps, which involves briefing an artist on the story and ordering appropriate visual material for a deadline. As well as handling individual stories, a reporter/producer might have to take responsibility for two or more programmes a day which involves determining the running order of the stories and coordinating the overall transmission of the broadcast.

18.00: If the programme is to be broadcast at 1900, by this time the producer must have a running order and write headlines which must be of a certain length to fit in with the titles. In determining the order of the packages, the reporter/producer must ensure the programme is balanced so, for example, that you don't go from death and destruction in Rwanda to a story about a skateboarding duck.

18.30: Close to going on-air, the reporter/producer moves into the gallery, the control centre for the programme, where there is a director, a director's assistant, a vision mixer, an auto-cue person, three camera operators, sound operator, Betacart operators who actually play the tape, and all of the VT (video-tape) editors who are cutting the packages. The producer has to make sure that everyone is aware of what is expected of them and take responsibility for the transmission of the programme.

Case study: reporter/producer, Sky News (24-hour rolling satellite/cable news channel)

It can be stressful if it's a busy day, if there's not enough editors, if the presenter is having an off day, if there's a technical problem, if reporters file late. Mostly the bulletin is ready to go by five to the hour. It's very high-paced. We work 12 hours a day and never stop. I've had to put packages together in 15 minutes from scratch and get them to air. But a lot of the time it's smooth and easy and you can sit and have a chat and a cup of tea.

There must be no duplication of stories, spokespeople must not crop up in more than one package, and ultimately everything must be timed correctly to the second and look as good as possible.

News and current affairs producers need a journalistic background or, if they are recruited from another area, a demonstrable interest in topical issues. A producer also has to have an understanding of others' roles and will usually have worked their way up from reporting.

Researcher

In broadcasting, research is one of the key roles in programme and package making. Researchers work right across the board, from light-entertainment where they check quiz questions and find competitors, to hard news and documentary where they research stories, arrange commentators, select music or archive footage and will find locations.

Working to the producer, the researcher gets ideas onto paper and prepares workable plans for the item. They must then research every aspect of the subject matter, find guests or spokespeople and initiate ideas. At the start of the day, the producer will brief the researcher on the item and it will be the researcher's role to find, say, a top doctor to come into the studio and comment on a new medical breakthrough. They will then make arrangements for transport and look after them throughout the programme. Journalistic experience is usually a prerequisite as researchers have to be able to work fast and effectively, knowing how to communicate their ideas and persuade people who may be nervous to participate. They also have to put their hands on facts instantaneously which can only come from experience and being aware of the world and well-read. Ultimately, what the producer wants is innovation. It's pointless creating a package about an issue in a way that has already been reported. Therefore it is up to the researcher to get a fresh angle and new spokespeople. A great deal of physical leg-work is involved. They will sometimes go out on location and assist directors and producers and will frequently act as their stand-in. Therefore it is a good route into production and reporting as researchers get to learn the intricacies of these roles first hand. A great deal of time is also spent on the telephone gathering information and organizing guests and spokespeople, scanning newspapers and checking press releases for new ideas. Researchers may also be required to liaise with item presenters, providing scripts and cues, so the ability to communicate on paper is also essential.

Far from being a glamorous job, it is hard and gruelling with very long, irregular hours. The benefits are that you get to learn the jobs of other practitioners and have opportunities to shape output.

Some researchers are specialists, particularly those working in the areas of science, finance or international affairs. A large proportion of researchers move from job to job because contracts are short to correspond with the life-span of a programme.

Therefore, researchers must demonstrate flexibility to apply themselves to the next task or subject.

Reporters

By far the greatest source of story ideas for any TV station should be its reporters. Most stations have a large complement of general staff reporters who, at a moment's notice, can turn their hand from covering a coup in a far-flung state to writing a package about a zoo's new arrival. Bigger stations might also employ specialist reporters who are expert in certain key areas, such as politics, science or business.

Investigative reporters are employed to expose wrongs or malpractice. Typically, they will work in a team on a documentary as opposed to a news bulletin or programme.

Most news television journalists, the vast majority of whom will have worked in print and radio beforehand, commence their broadcast career behind the scenes putting programmes together. It is essential that recruits understand the characteristics of television which make it such a fascinating journalistic medium. The work should not be seen as somehow inferior or subordinate to being on-camera because the majority of highly respected and experienced journalists never become household names. Going on-screen is simply a career choice or move, not necessarily a promotion.

The hours for any reporter are long and hard. Nights, weekends and bank holidays all have to be worked on top of completing stories which keep the reporter on the job or in the editing suite for many hours past home-time. On the plus side, the long hours tend to be balanced out by working on a shift basis. This means that while one week, the reporter might start at 5am on a Sunday morning, the following week they might not start till 2pm. Though they might not get home until past 3am! This at least explains why reporters tend to have a sense of humour as it acts as a motivational force when the going gets tough. TV is pressured enough so everyone has to pull together and see the funny side of life. The ability to stay calm and in control when you have 40 seconds before going on air and your package is still 20 seconds short is essential! The TV reporter is just one player in an accomplished, professional team which is why, despite the cliché of the foot-in-the-door hack, the majority of broadcast journalists are recruited for their affability.

Television journalists are usually very seasoned, accomplished print or radio reporters or even editors. They must have sufficient seniority to work independently and to direct their camera, sound and editing colleagues.

Off-screen journalists Working off-screen involves a wide variety of tasks which are designated by the news editor. For the news reporter these include researching stories to gather background information, establishing contacts who will be useful to a story, briefing interviewees so that they know what will be expected of them and when and where an interview will take place. There is also a major element of script and report writing to be done for transmission. More experienced off-screen journalists will deputize for the news editor where required, organizing location reports and providing their voice, but not their face, on items which have been shot without an on-screen reporter.

Organizing television news reports is clearly a demanding task. You have a lot of people to take into account, from your own colleagues to the people who are involved in your item. That means you have to be well-organized, persistent and have good interpersonal skills. Recording pictures can be time-consuming so you have to make sure your spokesperson feels relaxed as they may be giving up valuable time to take part in your interview.

On-screen journalists This role is the same as that of off-screen journalists with the addition that the on-screen journalist will present pieces-to-camera, which means they will physically deliver their report on-screen, conduct studio interviews and on-location reports. Having a journalist tell us face-to-face about an event or issue lends authority to the piece and wherever possible, a reporter will go on-screen. As the main communicator and mediator of the story to the audience, they must be skilled in presenting information in a clear and unambiguous way. Many complicated issues have to be clarified and analysed but in a style that is informative and accessible.

Limited airtime coupled with television's aim to bring news as it happens can place a great deal of pressure on on-screen journalists who sometimes, having arrived at an event just moments before broadcast, must report spontaneously live on-air without scripts. As well as reporting, these people have to direct the report, which means they guide the camera operator and think about the overall 'look' of the package, but without dictating to them! Teamwork is vital when faced with a tight schedule. They also work with video-tape editors to ensure the item is packaged to present the story accurately and in a form which is fair to all sides involved and clearly comprehensible to the viewer. It must also be the right length to within around three seconds as stipulated by the news editor. If the story is too long or too short, the programme's running schedule may be disastrously disrupted. Usually the reporter will be with a two-person crew of a camera-operator and sound recordist. The reporter will therefore need to liaise closely with the technical staff and supervise what is filmed and how the shots should look to the viewer.

Good looks are not the passport to a presentation job as many of the faces we see each day will testify! But authority coupled with a personable appearance and personality are essential if the audience is to feel comfortable and continue to tune in.

Case study: on-screen reporter, BBC regional station

The toughest yet most thrilling thing I find about my job is waking up very early in the morning and not having a clue what I'll be faced with that day. You have to be prepared to don any number of hats, from bright and cheerful coverage about the great British banger to solemn reporting on the death of a leading local light, all in the space of a few hours. All journalists come to expect it, especially in print journalism where reporters might write ten different stories a day but going on-screen to deliver the story carries the challenge of having to physically switch to an appropriate mood to set the right tone for thousands of viewers.

This journalist was one of the lucky few who managed to land his first job in television straight from university after graduating in Politics. Because this reporter had no prior print or radio experience, he underwent intensive journalistic and technical tuition as part of his overall training.

Like so many I applied for a BBC training scheme and promptly forgot about it because so many apply for so few places. I was up against very stiff competition from media graduates with fabulous showreels while all I had to show

for my abilities was a rolled-up copy of the university magazine. What worked in my favour was my specialist interest in
local government and probably my incredibly plain face. I
think looks play more of a role in commercial television
which is more glossy in appearance generally. The faces you
see on BBC programmes tend to look more lived in to lend
authority to what they are saying rather than distracting
from the message.

He says that any glamour associated with being seen on
television soon wears off.

I have been doing this job for eight years now and I assure
you my main priority is to tell the story to the best of my
ability with the best-looking pictures. I spend around 15 minutes per day talking to the camera which amounts to just
seconds on air. Any egotist would quickly find themselves
very bored indeed if that thrill was all they did the job for.

Correspondents

This is the romantic mecca of those who want to be television
journalists and is one of the most sought after positions in
journalism. Foreign correspondents may be based in cities
around the world where they become familiar with the local way
of life and file regular reports by telephone or using satellite
equipment to beam footage and voice reports back to the studio.
This is not a job for someone starting out in journalism; the
majority have worked their way to the top and have sufficient
seniority to be able to work independently in the field and be the
nation's eyes and ears abroad. While it may seem glamorous to
be based in some far-flung sunny climate, it is in fact one of the
toughest jobs in journalism, especially when covering a nation
divided by civil unrest. Correspondents face censorship of their
reports by the host state and may be physically monitored or
even, in extreme cases, intimidated if they report in a way which
displeases anyone involved.

It can also be tremendously rewarding to be one of the first to
witness an event and relay it to the rest of the world. Many
foreign correspondents are in the position of bringing suffering
out into the open which has spurred many charitable efforts.

These journalists must have an in-depth awareness of the affairs of the country they are working in and both the sensitivity and assertiveness to deal with red tape. Whereas their counterparts in the newsroom might work a 12-hour shift then go home, the foreign correspondent works whenever a story happens. If that means working several weeks on the frontline of a war, sleeping in mud and eating dried rations, so be it.

Newscasters/presenters

The majority of newsreaders are experienced journalists who have an active role in the newsmaking process. They certainly don't just sit around and wait to be handed their script on the hour! Their scripts may be prepared for them by colleagues but most presenters will play a part in writing and editing their own copy. The impeccable presenter you see on screen may look calm and in control, but the audience does not see any of what is going on in the background. The reader is wearing a talkback earpiece through which, for instance, they are updated on timing by the director in the control room and may be told to hurry up to make way for a last minute item or to slow down if the programming schedule gets changed. The activity on the studio floor and the hot, bright lights only add to the tension. In fact it is a wonder the presenters can hear themselves speak. Some have been known to comment after a bulletin that they do not remember what they have said. However, the high-pressure atmosphere is one of the things that can make news presenting so appealing in that it is exciting to know you are bringing the first details of an issue to millions of people. The adrenalin cannot fail to flow.

Presenters need to be authoritative and have a strong presence on-camera, their voices have to be strong and distinctive to keep the viewer's attention and their appearance should be presentable without being distracting. Outrageous hairstyles or unusual clothes would distract the viewer from what the presenter is saying. Likewise, fidgeting, excessive facial movements or gesticulation is also going to hamper the audience's concentration on the information being imparted.

In a few circumstances actors are hired exclusively for news presentation because they reflect the right image for the bulletin or organization. Their appearance combined with their trained voice commands the attention of the viewer whereas a skilled journalist who can write excellent scripts might not have good intonation or delivery. Actors will have their scripts prepared for them and will not contribute to newsgathering, but they will be encouraged to bring their presentation expertise to the fore by altering wording to make it more suitable for reading aloud.

The presenter reads from an auto-cue, which is a television screen rolling the script close to the camera so it looks as if the presenter is speaking directly to the viewer. The newsreader also has back-up from a written script.

Whereas the big news networks may have dedicated newsreaders, regional stations run a rota system so that reporters also read the news. In the case of documentaries or investigative programmes, the reporter is also likely to act as presenter.

Those are some of the main journalistic roles in television stations. But those people could not do their jobs without the following staff whose work is briefly described here. As journalists spend much of their time working as part of a team, it is vital they have an understanding of their roles.

Director

The director is concerned with the actual making of the programme or package and must have a clear understanding of the jobs of everyone involved. On location, or in the studio, they direct the crew and presenters or guests then, where applicable, guide the film and video editors. It is a creative role concerned with the overall 'look', style and continuity of the broadcast. It is unusual to find directors working on small news packages. That role is usually filled by the reporter. But they will be employed on documentaries which have a great deal more footage to shoot and where a large amount of material has to be conveyed in a way that will keep the audience on the edge of their seats for half an hour or more.

Directors need to be tactful team leaders who can cope with pressure and motivate others. They have to be able to communicate their ideas articulately to others they work with, particularly in the gallery. They do not need journalistic experience but should be knowledgeable enough about current affairs to be able to mediate these issues to an audience. Many directors cut their teeth in theatre and may move into film or television working in drama or light entertainment before moving into journalism.

Floor manager

This is a demanding role both physically and mentally, involving long, irregular hours both in and out of the studio and on location. The floor manager's role is basically to ensure the smooth running of the programme's production, such as timing, safety and supervision of camera, sound and other technical crew members. Based in the studio behind the cameras, they act as the link between directors and producers seated in the gallery or control room and the presenters or performers on the studio floor. Floor managers are equipped with two-way microphones so that they can receive instruction from the gallery to help convey the director's wishes to those working in the studio, therefore tact and diplomacy are essential. News readers and presenters are already under pressure or may, in some cases, have different ideas from the director over how they should speak. Floor managers also have to relay instructions to studio crew. They may in some cases be assisted by assistant floor managers or floor assistants who accurately notate all changes to scripts and ensure any guests are briefed and looked after. Floor managers usually begin their careers as trainee floor assistants who work their way up over four to five years. Direct entry to floor management is rare. Many television floor managers have experience in theatre production where they are required to work in a 'live' environment. Journalistic experience is not a prerequisite.

Production assistant

If you have ever been in the gallery as a news programme is broadcast, it is often the production or director's assistant's voice you hear chanting 10 ... 9 ... 8 ... as the countdown to transmission. PAs, as they are abbreviated, work in both television and radio providing administrative support. They schedule meetings, type scripts and keep accurate records as a programme is made. PAs often come from secretarial backgrounds and sometimes progress into research. Like most jobs in TV, role distinctions are blurred. Hours are long and irregular. Typing and shorthand skills are often required.

Graphic designer

The graphic designer's primary role is to produce clear, informative graphics, such as maps, charts and animated reconstructions, to illustrate and complement news stories. They must be able to interpret a brief (instructions) accurately to tight deadlines, liaising with producers to come up with the best effect. An interest in news and current affairs is essential, also flexibility as stories are so varied, from inflation to science. Creativity is important and the ability to push available technology to its limits. As well as working on story graphics, graphic designers also work on longer-term projects such as the general image of a programme or bulletin which involves anything from designing the set to making suggestions for the title sequence. They therefore work not only with pictures but with text so typographical expertise is important. Working patterns vary according to which programme the designer is working on. Night and weekend working is inevitable; you work as long as it takes to finish the job. Most television designers have a degree in graphic design. Prospects are good, with the possibility of promotion to management level where the designer could be in charge of the entire department and its output.

Camera operators

They work on location and in the studio and need both technical and creative ability to get the best from their camera equipment, filters and lenses. Working to the director, they convey their ideas onto tape. They usually have a background interest in the visual arts and begin their careers as junior operators and work their way up. Most operators specialize in their field, for instance wildlife, and many go freelance.

Case study: freelance camera operator and editor for Reuters, Sky, GMTV and Granada News

After taking a vocational course in TV and radio technical work, PW used wedding videos and training films as a lever into television. He says: 'I got into TV by accident. I happened to be with a friend at the Reuters office in Manchester when the Strangeways prison riot story broke and the reporter for Sky needed a camera operator. Now I cover mainly news and features.'

He says he uses journalistic skills to determine what shots will best illustrate the reporter's words, but is constantly looking at his watch: 'You are always fighting a deadline and you

can be called out at a moment's notice for a news company.'
The report begins by shooting establishing shots or GVs (general views). Then pieces-to-camera, where the reporter talks
into the camera, and interviews are recorded.
He explains:

> You have to think journalistically but in pictures as opposed
> to words. You also have to ascertain how long they want the
> final package to be so you shoot enough but not too much.
> On a few occasions where I have been called out and set up
> the camera I've had to do the interview myself, briefed from
> the newsroom in London as to what questions to ask but my
> voice has not been on air.

Once the footage has been shot, the job is not over. He
continues:

> With some television companies, when I have finished filming I hand the tape over to the reporter or a dispatch rider
> who takes it back to the studio to be edited. With others you
> also have to edit. For GMTV it's a little less rushed because
> they go out in the morning. With Sky, because they are a 24-
> hour news station, they are wanting packages all the time
> on-the-hour and occasionally you have to update with new
> material if it is an on-going story so you're filming and editing all the time. The pace and speed is very tight.

He insists working in television journalism is not as glamorous as people think.

> There is a tendency for people outside the industry to think
> that because it is TV. It's hard work. In the summer it's fine
> because you are out in the sunshine filming, but in winter
> when you are stood outside filming for hours on end it can be
> cold wet, long, hard hours.

Sound recordists

Sound operators, or recordists as they are often known, work
both on location and in the studio although crew numbers are
being cut and camera operators often find themselves doing the
sound operator's job, too. Sound quality plays a vital role in
every package or programme, not least in news where clarity is

vital. These people are technically skilled in the use of microphones and other equipment so they will know how to get the
best results in a force nine gale!

Picture/film/VT editors
These people work with the reporter, director or producer to edit
the package physically using highly sophisticated equipment.
Editors have to work extremely fast to tight deadlines as journalists always want to insert the latest information before a show
goes on air

While these job descriptions would appear to suggest roles are
clear-cut in television journalism, in reality the distinctions
between occupations are blurred. This is in no small part due to
the pressures that those in this medium are working under
because if something needs doing fast, such as finding a guest or
a piece of archive footage, any available person must be able to
get on with the task. It is a characteristic of all the media that in
order to succeed the journalist needs to be a good all-rounder, a
versatile self-starter who operates well in a team environment.

NEW AND FUTURE DEVELOPMENTS IN
TELEVISION JOURNALISM

A former editor of the *Nine O'Clock News* who set up BBC's
Breakfast Time news operation, says working practices and structures have been transformed within broadcasting. He worked in
broadcasting for 28 years but does not think anyone who is starting today stays in broadcasting full-time for that long any more.

Today, the whole culture has changed. New organizational
structures and rationalization mean successful broadcasters have
to be flexible. They have to be prepared to move around physically from one place to the next and stay for as little as three
months at a time and they have to equip themselves constantly
with the latest skills to stay ahead of competition for fewer jobs.
For example, television journalists now sometimes have to be
able to edit pictures, once the preserve of highly trained technical
experts but now made easier by technological advancement.
Reporters going on location will also increasingly find themselves assisting with lighting and sound recording. As in the
print industry, technological developments such as cable and

satellite have led to greater competition which has had the knock-on effect of leading station management to tighten staffing and production budgets.

There is a definite feeling within the industry and viewership that formats are getting a bit stale. The idea of having a familiar household name in a suit telling us about the news is a very British institution. It unites the nation before bedtime in a fairly authoritative way and, despite seeing and hearing graphic reports of tragedy, we all sleep soundly in the knowledge that, finally, the cat trapped in the baggage hold of an aeroplane has been safely rescued. To counteract this, even the most familiar daily programmes are now questioning their production values and subtly incorporating more sophisticated methods of presenting news. Highly trained graphic designers have always worked in television news, and now they are being employed to produce highly sophisticated computer graphics to accompany stories and also working on innovative sets to create the right mood or backdrop for the stories and presentation to be set against. They are also experimenting with different formats for presenting information, such as incorporating text with moving images on screen.

Designers are essential in that journalists, particularly those who have come from a radio background, cannot always envisage stories pictorially. But on the other hand, many graphic designers do not have sufficient news judgment to be able to present the information effectively. In the future, it is envisaged news formats will be less documentary-based and will incorporate graphics and text on screen in more innovative ways. A multi-media generation has grown up feeling very at ease with on-screen information, capable of synthesizing facts as they fly across the monitor, confident about gleaning details from text, pictures and sound all at the same time.

In the future, journalists will have to learn to present information in a graphic way and designers will have to develop more news sense so that both areas work in harmony.

The latest technological advances in television transmission involve satellite and cable. The main impact of satellite television has been to make programming international. Viewers in the UK can receive programmes from throughout Europe and sometimes further afield. The effect of journalism has been profound. You only have to think back to the Gulf War and the dramatic live footage of Allied jets on the first sorties over Baghdad. But there is a great deal of scope for making television local.

A cable system is basically a means of delivering television to the home via a network of coaxial copper or optical fibre cables installed beneath roads and pavements. The cable is connected to viewers' television sets, delivering channels from satellites and other sources. Systems currently being used can carry more than 40 channels and avoid the need for satellite dishes. The channels received by the viewer can be controlled so consumers can subscribe to some channels and not others. Cable television is described as a local delivery service because it delivers television channels within a specified area. Cable franchises so far granted cover around two-thirds of the UK's population with many already in operation.

Every cable and local delivery operator needs at least two licences – one for the system itself and the other for providing the cable programme or local delivery service – and a few need three if using wireless cable. Just one franchise is issued per area simply because of the cost and inconvenience of digging up roads and pathways to lay the cable. The ITC advertises a specific area and invites bids from companies. The exception is when the cable system can only serve 1000 homes or less or is confined within a single building, such as in the case of a university TV station. Then the operator normally needs no licence.

Interactive services, such as home banking and shopping and even meter reading are possible through cable. This has major implications for our everyday lives and is the subject of controversy. Critics fear we are heading towards an armchair-based culture where technology will allow us to perform most functions and duties without ever leaving our homes and communicating face-to-face with other people. Even a chat with neighbours as we buy a pint of milk at the corner shop will become a thing of the past. However, supporters of this kind of technology-led existence believe being able to perform mundane tasks such as bill-paying in seconds will free up more time for quality pursuits.

While technology offers the scope to speculate wildly about how we may live our lives in the future, what is irrefutable today is that the growth of video, cable and satellite channels means that the capacity of broadcasting to attract mass audiences regularly for any type of programme is becoming redundant.

Combined, this technology will spread viewing over more channels which could mean reduced viewing figures all round. The
implication is that budgets for certain types of programmes, such
as investigative reporting in commercial news programmes, will
be cut because advertising revenue will have to be shared with
all the new stations.The public sector's static but secure licence
fee should ensure that its resources are not so insecurely
depleted.

At the end of the day, it takes someone with that extra inde-
finable 'something' who can embody the skills and attributes
essential to a career in television journalism. If you think that you
have 'it', read on for some training opportunities.

7

Broadcast journalism: training and entry routes

Broadcast journalists tend to enter the industry by one of four main routes:

1. full-time pre-entry course;
2. from a career in print journalism;
3. by working in another broadcasting job then transferring to journalism;
4. in-house training schemes.

FULL-TIME PRE-ENTRY COURSE

This is the main route into broadcast journalism for 'beginners'. A pre-entry course is one which is taken before the candidate embarks on a career in journalism but does not automatically guarantee a job. Among the most popular and respected courses are those offered by the National Council for the Training of Broadcast Journalists (NCTBJ) although others are being set up which are advertised in the national press. These courses vary in length and content. In addition, a number of undergraduate degrees are being established which offer journalism and/or broadcasting as an option. Before we look at these other courses, let us first examine the NCTBJ more closely.

The NCTBJ is made up of voluntary representatives from organizations throughout the radio and television industry, the National Union of Journalists and a range of educational establishments offering journalism training. The council's role is to liaise closely with colleges to ensure key standards are met and to advise on course structure and content. NCTBJ recognized courses vary in structure and length as the Council recognizes or is in the process of recognizing a variety which include:

- one-year full-time diploma courses;

- two-year Higher National Diploma courses;

- three-year undergraduate degree courses;

- one or two-year postgraduate diplomas.

Course titles and the list of institutions offering them is constantly changing. For an up-to-date list, contact the NCTBJ's secretary: Gordon Parker, 188 Lichfield Court, Sheen Road, Richmond, Surrey, TW9 1BB. Tel/Fax 0181 940 0694.

Whatever the format or level of the course, in order to obtain NCTBJ accreditation it must deliver the following:

- technical skills and practical training in news editing and writing;

- interview techniques;

- bulletin preparation;

- media law;

- public administration;

- journalistic practices and ethics.

If the training forms part of a degree, there will be further elements to the course such as media theory or business practice. Many courses now offer a period of work placement varying in length from a couple of weeks to a whole term.

While the courses have a successful track record and have helped launch countless careers, there is no guarantee of a job at the end of it.

Fees vary according to the type and duration of the course. Some local authority grants are available or colleges may have details of sponsorship. Many students write directly to companies asking for funding.

To find out what degrees include broadcast skills, and in what capacity, look through the *UCAS Handbook,* which is available in careers offices and libraries, and which lists every course and institution in the UK. Contact colleges and universities directly for a prospectus.

The vice-chairman of the National Council for the Training of Broadcast Journalists (NCTBJ) and former Head of Journalism Training at the BBC has seen many of his former students become top household names. He believes a graduate will tend to be favoured because they have demonstrated that they have analytical skills and can marshal facts which is of great value to journalism. He thinks degrees that demonstrate this best are political, historical, geographical or scientific. Media courses have the benefit of often being well-equipped in terms of technology. Good courses, and they do vary in quality, concentrate less on button-pushing and encourage students to be multi-skilled and creative.

According to the NCTBJ, the industry looks favourably at courses which are structured in such a way that they understand the industry and have good contacts within it. This type of course tends to offer students work placements which can be crucial to their career.

However, one television news producer says that for the would-be journalist, the technical introductions to camera work and editing often obtained on degrees can be undesirable. She thinks the most useful thing you can have is a language because most people at the station where she works have two. By far the most used, she says, are German, French and Spanish. Science can be useful if that is needed for a science programme but unlikely to be used on a day-to-day basis. Most of all, she stresses, there's no point in learning how to be a VT editor or vision mixer because other people have made that their skill. In fact it can annoy the experts when someone inexperienced claims to know how to do it.

It is important to find out who is teaching the course and how much industrial experience they have. Ask whether they encourage visiting lecturers who are currently working in the industry to teach on the course. Good courses also incorporate a period of work experience which is organized by the student with assistance from tutorial staff. An important question to ask is what proportion of graduates gain work in the industry. Educational institutions cannot be made responsible for ensuring their students get jobs, especially when graduate unemployment is high, but those colleges and universities which have good links with the industry often pave the way to successful broadcasting careers.

Keep an eye out for other courses advertised in the national press. Alternatively, your local college may offer a relevant course so call for a prospectus.

VIA PRINT JOURNALISM

Local BBC and ILR stations offer in-house training to journalists who have been recruited from a print media background. This will cover such technical areas as recording, editing, writing for radio and voice training. Many broadcast journalists begin their careers in newspapers so refer to Chapter 4 on print journalism training for details about courses and other entry routes.This can be frustrating for those hoping to make an early launch into the industry, but successful candidates tend to have supplemented their print experience by working for news agencies or radio stations in their spare time. It is standard practice to have a minimum of three years' journalistic experience in print and preferably some radio. While many make the transition successfully, certain print journalists adapt more readily to broadcast. These are ones who are dedicated to broadcast journalism and can think how they would treat stories with the added dimensions of sound and pictures. They must have boundless energy, be self-motivated and have the kind of voice or presence to give them authority on screen or over the airwaves.

TRANSFER FROM OTHER BROADCASTING JOBS

There are plenty of examples of people working in radio newsrooms who have worked their way in from other departments. There is no doubt that being in the right place at the right time can help enormously. You get to hear about vacancies and opportunities before they are ever advertised and know key personnel involved. Editorial assistants frequently find their way into journalism. They are often called upon to voice pieces and get to know the work of journalists and the organization of the newsroom intimately, often better than journalists themselves.

The BBC runs an attachment scheme for internal staff.They apply and are interviewed for the attachments which can range from three months to a year in another department. During the

attachment, they basically work for another department or programme from their own in whatever capacity they are assigned.
The aim is to give candidates broad experience and new skills to
enhance their regular work.

BROADCAST JOURNALISM: TRAINING SCHEMES

The BBC and ITV run trainee schemes now and then which are
bi-media posts, that is the trainee works in both radio and television. They are advertised as and when staffing levels permit or
demand for them is sufficient. These traineeships are fixed-term
paid staff jobs during which the successful applicant works as a
journalist while undertaking intensive and extensive training.
The number of places offered is therefore limited and competition is understandably fierce. There is no guarantee of further
employment at the end of the contract but you have a clear
advantage over others without this experience. Preference is
given to graduates who have already demonstrated a practical
commitment to journalism through work experience or through
prior training on a one-year full-time postgraduate course.
Training is given mainly by experienced journalists who may still
be working in the industry. Course content varies but broadly
covers the following areas:

- news writing and editing;
- technical skills;
- media law;
- interviewing methods;
- government and politics.

Here is just a selection of some of the schemes available but there
are others. Contact personnel departments for details of individual companies' schemes, where they exist.

BBC News Trainee Scheme

A few places are available each year for graduates to join the
BBC's News Trainee Scheme which, in keeping with the BBC's bi-
media policy, trains journalists for both television and radio. The
scheme is theoretically open to new graduates but, in reality,

those who have some professional media experience or who have already completed a year's formal training course tend to have more chance of getting in.

BBC Journalist Trainee Scheme, established in 1970, offers about 12 people a year professional training in radio and television News and Current Affairs. Each course last two years with work placements in different areas of the BBC's journalistic output both in radio and television. The BBC's Regional News Training Scheme was launched in 1989 and is again mainly bimedia oriented. It runs in the same way as the national scheme but on a local level.

Formal Basic Broadcasting Training takes place in London and lasts around four months. This covers BBC editorial policy and principles, media law, visits, talks and technical tuition. Rigorous selection procedure includes interviews, written news knowledge, news-writing ability and voice tests.

Qualifications/requirements

- degree or equivalent;
- knowledge and understanding of current events;
- lively enquiring mind;
- proven journalistic or relevant experience which suggests genuine interest in or commitment to broadcast journalism;
- those selected expected to become proficient in shorthand and typing before they start their traineeship.

For the Regional Scheme, additional requirements include:

- enthusiasm for BBC Local Radio;
- prepared to work and travel anywhere;
- current full driving licence.

BBC Television Production Trainee Scheme

This two-year scheme involves learning about programme making. Competition is tough – 6000 applicants for ten places is the norm – and training is demanding and there is no guarantee of a job at the end of it. But by the end you will have a firm grasp of

TV production which will stand you in good stead for applying for job contracts as researcher or assistant producer. The scheme starts with a short induction course followed by placements to specific programmes with on-the-job training. Trainees are required to take the initiative when it comes to securing these placements which could be anywhere within the network, including children's TV, community programmes unit, drama, light entertainment or features.

Qualifications/requirements

- educated to at least A-levels but preferably with a degree or substantial experience in the media;

- one year's work experience (minimum) in the media;

- fascination with TV and the ability to think visually;

- good interpersonal skills;

- innovative ideas and a good grasp of current affairs.

BBC Network Radio Production Trainee Scheme

This scheme is not for reporters or presenters but for would-be producers. It could be a good way in. The two-year programme is competitive – 900 applicants for ten jobs – and there is no guarantee of work at the end. The first five weeks are with BBC Radio Training, providing an introduction to the BBC as a whole and training in basic technical radio skills and dummy programme-making. The course also covers writing for radio and basic law for journalists. After this, there follow three-month working attachments organized for you to a variety of departments, mainly London-based, primarily to speech-based factual programming departments.

Qualifications/requirements

- at least 22 years old;

- for people who want to produce factual speech programmes;

- producers need to be articulate and gregarious and able to work easily with people of all kinds;

- a wide range of interests;

- fascinated by what's going on in the world;
- technically capable with good writing skills;
- physically and mentally tough.

BBC World Service Production Trainee Scheme

This scheme involves two years' comprehensive training and experience in radio production in the World Service, with normally only three trainees recruited from 800 applicants. Training consists of formal instruction leading to direct work experience on a number of programmes. Formal courses are London-based although trainees will also work in another part of the UK for a limited period. While undertaking their training, candidates are based in one of a number of departments including World Service in English, scriptwriting units or one of the language services.

Qualifications/requirements

- political awareness;
- overseas work experience and specialist knowledge of another part of the world;
- informed interest in international affairs;
- writing ability, broadcasting-quality voice and plenty of ideas.

The BBC advertises all vacancies open to external applicants in the national press and a summary appears on CEEFAX. Contact BBC Corporate Recruitment Services, London W1A 1AA.

Granada Trainee Programme Maker Scheme

Granada Television is the longest established independent commercial television company in the UK whose broadcasting record includes *Coronation Street*, *World in Action* and *Prime Suspect*. Their main training opportunity is the Trainee Programme Maker Scheme. Intake is limited and depends on resources. In 1994, three trainee programme makers were employed. Granada say they are looking for a small number of high-calibre people with enthusiasm, creativity and energy to contribute from day one to programme making ranging from entertainment to current affairs, sport and drama.

Training covers the following areas:

1. initial assignment as a trainee researcher on a studio-based programme, where they will observe how such a programme is made and develop ideas for inclusion; they will shadow and assist researchers and producers;
2. single camera training to learn how to deliver short items or inserts;
3. periods spent in entertainment, local and factual departments where the candidate will broaden their research and production experience into other areas of programming;
4. subsequent assignment as a researcher to a specific programme for practical on-the-job training.

As candidates gain experience, they are eligible to apply for producers' courses and studio director courses run each year.

Qualifications

- a good degree although the subject is unimportant;

- flair, creativity and commitment.

Vacancies are advertised nationally in July. Selection is rigorous consisting of written tasks, workshops and individual interviews. Contact: Personnel Department, Granada Television, Quay Street, Manchester M60 9EA.

Reuter's Journalist Trainee Scheme

This graduate training scheme lasts two-and-half years with successful candidates progressing to become staff journalists. Since September 1994 Reuters has been concentrating on recruiting trainees to its financial sector. Recruits undergo intensive practical training for seven weeks in London to give a basic foundation in fast, accurate news writing. Then, based at their London newsrooms, they undertake work experience on economics news desks. Training also includes general news and television techniques.

Qualifications/requirements

- a degree;

- a keen interest in international financial markets;

- specialist knowledge of economic journalism or financial analysis not essential but an advantage;

- background in economics, statistics or mathematics preferred;

- fluency in at least one foreign language helpful.

Contact: Personnel Department (Graduate Recruitment), Reuters Limited, 85 Fleet Street, London EC4P 4AJ.

It cannot be stressed enough how tough competition is to gain a place on these and other trainee schemes as not only do they significantly enhance your chances of being kept on for a job upon completion but you are also paid a salary for the duration of the scheme. It can be argued, however, that journalists should gain a breadth of experience during their training which cannot be best achieved while attached to one particular organization. Whatever route you take, remember that potential employers are going to be looking for a lot more than just paper qualifications. Communication skills, news knowledge and how you work in a team are additional qualities to enhance to your advantage. Good luck.

8

Agencies, freelancing and public relations

By now it is evident that being a journalist means a whole lot more than being employed by a specific media organization. It is a vocation, a culture, a way of being that permeates every aspect of the practitioner's life. Journalists tend to move around a lot from company to company and do not always stay within the mainstream media. They relish the challenge of utilizing their skills in various capacities. In this section, we will look at news-gathering and newsmaking organizations which employ journalists and which do not directly publish or broadcast themselves but instead **service** those industries.

NEWS AGENCIES

News agencies such as Reuters, Associated Press and the press Association supply news, features and pictures to different news organizations spanning all types of media. The arrangement may vary from, for example, a newspaper or television station paying the agency a yearly retainer to supply unlimited text, images and footage, or the agency offering copy or other material on a specu-lative basis, which means the agency is paid per item used. Some agencies are primarily international, for instance Reuters and Universal News Services. Among the top national agencies are the Press Association and Associated Press, who are also expand-ing to provide foreign coverage.

On a smaller scale, there are many local or specialist agencies dotted around the country, including News Team in Birmingham and Mercury in Liverpool. They vary in size from hundreds of

employees providing copy on world events to a one- or two-person
crew covering a local magistrates court.

Any agency relies very much on selling its work to a newspaper or broadcasting organization. Unlike radio or TV news
programmes or newspapers, agencies cannot rely on the licence
fee, cover price or advertising for income. They make all their
money from selling stories so they tend to be fiercely competitive
with each other and the news media and will pull out all the
stops to supply an exclusive. They aim to beat staff reporters of
newspapers or broadcasting organizations to a story so that they
can charge them for it.

News agencies have a strong reputation for being breeding
grounds for national journalists because they encourage tenacity,
perseverance and motivation on the part of their recruits.
Journalists working for agencies are prepared to go to any
lengths to get a picture or story, especially for the tabloid market.
But agencies are not just about supplying sordid scoops,
although these kinds of stories do earn them lots of money.
Agencies are also an important source of 'bread-and-butter'
copy, such as court and council reports, and will be commissioned by newspaper, radio and television newsdesks to cover
events that they don't have enough available staff to cover.
Agencies are used especially by regional newspapers for national
and international stories as a local paper cannot afford to post a
reporter miles away.

Agencies are a good stepping stone for reporters hoping to
work in a range of media because they often have to supply copy
and tapes to radio and television stations as well as written copy
to newspapers. Some agencies are specifically oriented towards
the broadcast industry including IRN which provides copy and
audio to independent local and national radio, and Reuters TV
which supplies footage and packages to television.

The agency newsroom

The newsroom of an agency operates and is structured in almost
exactly the same way as that of a newspaper or television
station. The only difference is that they do not have printing
presses and do not broadcast direct to the public. Everything
they do is sent to their clients, mostly digitally, to their computer
database down a telephone line. In terms of personnel, they have

editors, journalists and sub-editors, photographers and television crews and technical support in the agencies that provide television footage. They may also employ graphic artists if they offer that kind of service.

Journalists working for agencies may have to liaise directly with the newsdesks of their clients if they have been commissioned to provide something specific. If they are the type of agency that supplies exclusives to tabloids, there may be a degree of negotiation to be undertaken over fees and other matters, which is usually done by the newsdesks or picture editors of both the agency and the client.

The newsdesk operates like any other – prospects are planned ahead and reporters are assigned to cover diary events, such as court cases, news conferences and any other major stories. These will then be distributed speculatively to clients, or the client will have contacted the agency and asked them to cover a story specifically for them for an agreed fee.

Working in an agency differs from working for a newspaper, radio or television directly in that there is a lesser guarantee that what you have worked on for hours or even days will be used. Many journalists thrive on being associated with their paper or station and build their reputation upon it, whereas except in the case of well-known and respected agencies, agency journalists can feel a little out on a limb with no real reporting identity.

Radio news agency employees sometimes comment that they miss working alongside other station staff such as disk jockeys as part of the community, helping to shape its identity. On the other hand, the chance to write for a broadsheet one day and write for a television news programme the next brings a variety of experience not found in a staff job and, according to those who do the job, the thrill of working with top national and international stories 24-hours a day cannot be surpassed.

Working for an agency commands considerable adaptability in terms of writing style. Your story might appear in a range of publications or be used in radio or television programmes so it must be equally attractive to all. You must not over-simplify or use tabloid language in a story which will also be sent to *The Times*. Therefore, unless the journalist knows their story will only be used by a specific client or sector, they write factually and precisely so that the copy can easily be adapted to suit the needs of the customer. Introductions are neither too short nor too long.

Language is accessible but rich in detail and not over-simplified with slang terminology.

Case study: Reuters

Reuters is one of the world's biggest news agencies which began by breaking stories with 'pigeon power'. Launched by Julius Reuter more than 140 years ago, Reuters used pigeons carrying written reports to bridge gaps in telegraph lines as a way of circulating news and information fast. Today, the company uses some of the most sophisticated electronic technology, such as satellites, to supply news and television services to the world's media.

This agency employs a network of approximately 1200 journalists, photographers and camera operators based at 120 bureaux in 74 countries gathering information for newspapers and broadcasting organizations. They also supply a wide range of other services including statistics for the business and finance world.

Reuters World Service is an English-language general news service for print and broadcasting. Still pictures from around the globe are transmitted digitally straight onto their computer screens. They also provide graphics with accompanying text in several languages. Reuters television breaks news in 81 countries using satellite equipment. TV companies subscribe to the service and include its coverage in their bulletins.

Agency reporters may find themselves covering a football match in France, scientific research in Siberia or a natural disaster in Asia. Many Reuters reporters in the more remote districts carry portable satellite telephone equipment consisting of a dish and special telephone which can run off a car battery which may be the only available source of power for hundreds of miles. They would then telephone through their report to a copytaker at one of the bureaux worldwide.

News 200 is the name of the delivery system Reuters uses to supply information to newsdesks. Colour-coded, it allows editors quickly to select desired items off the screen. Most of Reuters' subscribers will automatically receive every piece of copy produced for a yearly fee.

As well as supplying text and pictures, both still and moving, Reuters has recently launched a radio news service to rival IRN.

News agencies: training and entry routes

Recruitment to agencies is very much the same as for mainstream papers and broadcast stations. Local agencies will take on people who have done pre-entry courses and a few may recruit individuals whom they train. Some, particularly the big reputable agencies, will only recruit experienced journalists. Reuters, on the other hand, operates a graduate trainee scheme for foreign television journalism correspondents (details under broadcasting in-house schemes, p. 179). Many agencies will offer work placements which can lead to employment. These vary in availability so you must contact the agency directly for information. Be aware that the nature of the work is highly demanding and not for the faint-hearted. As discussed earlier, stories sometimes have to be obtained against all odds!

While working for an agency offers diversity and a semblance of security, some journalists choose to operate independently and work for themselves.

FREELANCE JOURNALISM

It is a fact of life that more and more people who work in the media operate on a freelance basis or on short-term contracts of as little as 12 weeks. The comparatively cheaper cost of employing people on a casual basis, which does not encumber the company with responsibility for administering and paying for sickness and holiday pay, for instance, is increasingly attractive as staff budgets are severed. For some journalists, this brings uncertainty and insecurity, especially if they have commitments such as mortgages. But for many, going freelance, that is working independently and not tied to one particular organization, can be highly lucrative and allow the journalist to work as and when they want and for a variety of different employers. There are many different kinds of freelances in all areas of the media including writers, photographers, camera operators and sub-editors. It is perhaps writers who have the most freedom and flexibility as they do not have to work in an office to do their job. The basic requirement is access to a telephone so they can literally provide copy wherever they may be. Freelance journalism is the way many journalists break into a full-time media career and accounts for up to 10% of all journalists. Freelances are either general reporters, that is they write on a host of issues and in a variety of styles, from hard news to fashion, or they are specialists, covering sport, women's issues, politics and everything else besides.

Many people who work outside the media, for example politicians, lecturers and artists, will work as a freelance journalist as a sideline to make some extra money and will offer unique expertise that a general staff reporter either cannot or does not have the time to research.

For freelance journalists working for newspapers or magazines, there are two main ways of working. Some publications hire freelances to work what is known as a shift. That means they are paid a flat fee to report, write features or sub-edit for a set number of hours at the office. Other print journalists are paid what is known as lineage where they are paid per story commissioned. This means they can work from home for as long as it takes to research and write the copy, as long as it reaches the editor before the deadline.

In broadcasting, similar work patterns occur for journalists while technical staff, for example sound people, camera operators and editors, will have to work as and when required at the appropriate location for the report.

It is no easy task starting up as a freelance from scratch. Even for the experienced, who have worked full-time and have a valuable directory of clients and contacts, it does not always make a living. Most will tend to work as a staffer for a good period of time before going it alone. Freelances working from a back bedroom have to compete with newspapers or broadcasting organizations to get the story first if they are going to be able to sell it. It takes a great deal of commitment and courage as well as hard work to keep ahead of competition and make a reputable name for yourself. As well as researching and writing stories, often at anti-social times such as Christmas Day, there is also the business side to deal with when you are a self-employed freelance. This means, for instance, keeping accounts, dealing with the Inland Revenue, chasing up payment and paying electricity and petrol bills. Unfortunately, being ill or taking a well-earned break can be costly as you do not have the back-up of holiday or sick pay in the same way that staff journalists do. You also have to be good at marketing your own skills and, on top of all this as a freelance you have to keep a steady supply of stories flowing if you are to be seen as a reliable source.

Freelances gather stories in the same way staff journalists do but are likely to have to work harder at it until they become established. This is because they do not initially have the authority of a well-known media organization. Freelances spend much of their time meeting people from all walks of life and building up their trust so that should a story arise, the contact will call them first. An established freelance may also be called by the newspaper or broadcaster who wants them to cover a story for them because it cannot be followed up from the office. For instance, an inquest may be taking place which they cannot spare a staff reporter to attend. This often happens out-of-hours or at weekends when staff complements are lower.

There are great benefits to going it alone as many freelances will testify. If you come up with a good story you can sell it many times over to interested media. News organizations vary in how much they pay but freelances they feel comfortable with and use regularly can usually negotiate more than the going rate. For someone selling a story for the first time, tabloids tend to pay better than quality newspapers. There is no set rate for payment. Much will depend on whether the story is exclusive, which means it is sold to one client alone, or whether it revolves around celebrities or VIPs. Freelances who are well-known to the commissioning organizations are also likely to command a higher fee. Basically, you can earn anything from £5 (the cost of a tip-off to a local radio station) to thousands for exclusive pictures of a member of the royal family.

If a freelance has work to offer, they will normally first approach the news editor, if it is news, or the features department by telephone with a brief synopsis of the story. The journalist will be careful not to give too much away as this might allow the prospective buyer to produce the story on its own to avoid paying the freelance. If the company is interested, they tend to do one of two things: they will either ask for the copy to be submitted 'on spec', meaning the contributor will not be paid unless the story is used, or they will commission it which means the freelance will get paid whether the story is used or not.

Established freelances often produce their work on computers with modems which allow them to transmit their stories electronically to the VDUs at the office in seconds. Others will dictate their copy to a copytaker. Radio freelances will pass audio by telephone lines which can give a raw immediacy to the report which many stations like. Magazine freelances can send in copy double-line spaced on A4 sheets of paper.

Magazines use a vast number of freelances to write features and will very occasionally advertise. In fact well over half the copy is supplied in this way. There are opportunities for specialists in emotional issues for the young person's glossy market, cookery, fashion, gardening, motoring and travel. Registers are kept of freelance journalists and several professional associations exist for specialists. Magazines can pay hundreds of pounds for a feature. For instance, one top national young women's magazine will pay £400 for 2000 words but that includes your expenses and is before tax.

Broadcast journalism is a smaller industry than print in terms of personnel and there are less freelance opportunities available, particularly for the inexperienced although openings do arise. Experienced radio and television reporters, newsreaders and technical operators can sometimes obtain shift work at quiet periods such as weekends and Christmas. Freelance writers will usually offer their work to radio and television as well as print as it pays better. To do this requires some skill in writing in the appropriate style for the spoken word which is normally more concise.

A freelance news camera operator says there are downsides to his role but many positive aspects, particularly being his own boss:

> One drawback is the travelling. In the North West you can cover as far up to Carlisle, Hull and down to North Wales, a vast area. The other insecurity is the freelance work itself and trying to get it. When jobs don't come in you don't get paid. I like the unpredictability. Most of the time you do know what you will do beforehand but something big may break. The money is good though you have to buy your own equipment.

Overall the chances of something big breaking for a freelance are just as high as for a journalist working as a seasoned staffer for a big company. As with all journalism, it is down to being in the right place at the right time and being alert enough to spot a story. Some journalists have the uncanny knack of walking into major stories when they least expect. Most will carry a notepad, camera or tape recorder even when they go on holiday on the off-chance something out of the ordinary will happen.

But for our next set of journalists, gathering stories is not enough. They want to make the headlines.

PUBLIC RELATIONS

It is a popular misconception that public relations, or PR, is a disreputable relation when compared with the more 'serious' work of the hard news reporter. This is based on the belief that those who work in this area spend much of their time unabashedly promoting organizations at cocktail parties for a large fee. Journalists working for print and broadcast organizations, on the other hand, consider their own role to be objective, not controlled by market forces, and therefore more reputable – a questionable assumption.

In reality, hospitality is only a small, and clearly more visible, part of the work of a public relations officer. Long gone are the days when press officers spent their days in hotel receptions rubbing shoulders with the rich and famous. Public relations is now at work in all parts of society, for a host of different organizations, both public and private, showing that PR is infinitely more complex and sophisticated than most people would imagine.

Public relations comes in many guises, for example, sometimes jobs or titles are listed under corporate communications, publicity, external affairs and customer relations to name but a few. Most PRs would say their working day incorporates most of those roles.

According to the latest figures, approximately 48 000 people work in PR in the UK at the moment. Growth in the number of PR jobs at all levels has been higher than that of any other management function over the past 15 years, according to the Institute of Public Relations (IPR), the PR industry's own public relations umbrella. This reflects the recognition of the importance of maintaining an organization's public profile through carefully considered and planned communication and corporate identity.

The official definition of PR cited by the IPR is: ... 'the planned and sustained effort to establish and maintain goodwill and mutual understanding between an organisation and its publics'. But perhaps a better way to think about PR is to write down a list of the names of the charities, brand names, personalities, companies or any other organization that first springs into your mind. Then ask yourself why you thought of them first. Do they have a clearly identifiable image? Do they seem approachable, human and friendly? Or do you just feel you know a lot of good things about them and what they do? If it's any of these, it's the result of a great deal of investment in securing a good public image through PR.

Breaking that somewhat dry, official definition down into its components reveals the scope of flexibility in this much misunderstood career.

The 'organization' can be a government body, a business, profession, charity perhaps concerned with the arts, environment, education or science – in fact any large or small corporate or voluntary organization. This means that some PR officers will cover a range of areas, particularly those working, say, in the busy press office of a local authority, while others will specialize in environmental issues or parliamentary affairs. Its 'public' refers to audiences that are vital to that organization, be it the media, customers, suppliers, investors and so on. The PR's role is to mediate between the organization and its public to ensure its sustained credibility.

There are two main types of public relations operation:

1. The in-house public relations department which operates solely to promote the interests of that particular organization. PR staff here need a good in-depth knowledge of that firm, its overall interests and mission and must win the trust and support of other management.
2. The public relations consultancy which may perform the public relations duties on behalf of a number of clients. This could mean promoting a car exhaust one day and a nightclub the next!

Today, it is rare for any medium or large firm not to have some kind of in-house or external public relations support. For those which operate an in-house system, the public relations personnel is increasingly becoming a senior part of the management team.

Role of PR

As stated earlier, the work of the public relations officer is by no means clearcut and it is certainly not just about the archetypal writing of press releases. It can incorporate a variety of activities and the practitioner has to be multi-skilled and flexible to deal with the changing nature of the company they represent. However, the following sections describe some of the activities public relations people are involved with.

Programme planning

Public relations is a meticulously planned and carefully executed business and a lot of the press officer's time is spent researching and preparing their programme of action for promoting, say, a company or an event. It involves identifying and analysing problems which may exist in terms of current strategies and suggesting and planning solutions to meet the overall objectives of the organization. This also includes budgeting and managing resources for the project such as printing leaflets or buying advertising space.

For example, let us imagine a hypothetical project for a press officer: A newly registered charity set up to protect bats has been launched. A press officer has been appointed to promote the cause. She addresses several challenges to overcome including the poor public image of bats, competition for funds with other charities and lack of finance. She realizes that to overcome the latter two problems, her initial objective will be a consciousness-raising exercise to make the potential bene-factors adopt a positive approach towards bats. Then, with a small fund, she can begin to spread the message wider by pro-ducing publicity material and events. So she has prioritized the need to obtain support from a small circle of sponsors initially, such as companies, to enable her to build up her campaign. But to reach those people, she needs to liaise with the media.

Media relations

The press officer must develop and maintain a good working relationship with print and broadcast media to help encourage them to publicize the organization they represent. This clearly means the press officer must have a good understanding of the workings of newspapers, magazines, radio and television on a local, national and international level. Cultivating relationships with individual editors, appreciating copy deadlines and having some media writing and production knowledge themselves aids in engendering a good relationship with the media.

Writing news releases targeted at newspapers, radio and television journalists, magazine articles for mainstream and trade publications, TV and radio scripts is all in a day's work for a successful press officer. They may also be involved with all aspects of production of brochures, videos and exhibitions. You may or may not need technical expertise in skills such as operating a camcorder, but what is vital is a precise notion of the audience you are working to and the organization you are working for so you know the message will get across.

Our press officer decides she must try to establish a working rapport with one journalist at each publication and station that she will be targeting in her campaign. She realizes that this method will have more impact and ensure coverage far more than approaching a different journalist each time she needs publicity. This is because the chosen contact will already know the charity's background and significance. Through various media directories, she notes the names and telephone numbers of each media organization within her catchment area, calls the newsroom and asks for the name of any journalists who might specialize in environmental issues. If there are no specialists, she will introduce herself to one member of the editorial staff and make a note of their name for future contact. Before she can send out any material, though, she must develop a strong visual identity for the charity so their press releases and letterheads stand out from the rest, increasing their chances of being used by journalists who receive publicity material by the sackload each week.

Corporate identity

Most firms want to promote a positive reputation or 'mood' rather than just to plug a product or a service. Research has shown that the public responds far better to messages or products to which a subtle image or promotion of a desirable ideology or lifestyle has been associated. This can be achieved through good design and written communication skills. Here again, a clear understanding of the target audience, which can only be achieved through in-depth research, is vital.

> Here, our press officer sets about researching her target audience and considers what kind of image the charity should project. She has a small amount of money in the form of a grant and decides it should be directed into developing a strong corporate identity as a means of attracting further funding. Rather than tackle a design brief herself, she calls upon a friend who has recently qualified as a graphic designer and is looking for commissions to build up a portfolio. The designer quizzes her in depth about the main message the charity is trying to project. He works on the project and, after several meetings, presents her with a package containing letterheads, press release paper and compliment slips. All of these can be cheaply photocopied.
>
> With her raw materials, she decides a good way of bringing potential benefactors together is to organize a special event.

Special events

All kinds of events take place to draw attention to an organization – news conferences, openings of premises or plays, VIP visits, competitions and many more. The PR has to plan and organize the events carefully and ensure the media receives every encouragement to cover the event by feeding them information about it through press releases, brochures and general hospitality! Obtaining media coverage has the effect of bringing the topic to the public's attention which, in the case of, say, a charity, can raise consciousness or funds for the concern involved. Events also give public relations officers the opportunity to make contact with journalists in person in the hope that they can cultivate future publicity.

> Our press officer decides a good gimmick would be to get local companies to sponsor a bat box to be hung in trees around woods. She writes letters to company managers and gains sup-

port for the scheme. Conscious of the persuasive power of the media, she sends out a press release promoting an event which would achieve publicity both for the charity and the firms involved which will increase their willingness to participate. She organizes a photo opportunity featuring a company manager up a ladder hanging a box in a tree. One of the bat group members will bring along some captive bats in the hope that when people see how small and harmless bats are, they might feel more sympathetic to their plight. The press officer invites all her contacts. However, she realizes that not all media organizations will attend so she invites a local photographer and prepares a press release to accompany pictures to be sent out immediately after the event to maximize the chances of coverage. It reads:

PRESS RELEASE: for immediate publication
Homeless bats get a helping hand

Local businesses are going batty in a bid to preserve endangered wildlife. Ten firms are each providing homes for the tiny, winged creatures whose habitat is protected by law.

Managers swapped their bowler hats for hard hats yesterday to hang purpose-built wooden boxes in trees in Stapleton Wood, Heston. The plea for help came from a new Heston-based charity, Save the Bat, whose mission is to highlight the plight of these misunderstood and maligned mammals.

Roger Nelson, who runs Nelson Spark Plugs in Turner Road, said: 'I'm happy to help. Bats get a raw deal because people don't think they are cute yet they are vital to the environment by keeping insect numbers down.'

The other nine firms giving a home to bats are [insert list].

Bats are an endangered species whose numbers and natural habitat are rapidly dwindling because of man-made hazards such as building developments and timber treatments. Save the Bat is a new registered charity set up to raise funds, increase public awareness and care for sick and injured specimens.

> **ENDS**
> **Note to Editors: for more information about Save the Bat,**
> **contact the press office on 0166 62626.**

Mechanics

Other routine daily tasks for PR people include:

1. Compiling and updating press mailing lists so that promotional material is sent to individual journalists by name. This enhances the likelihood of the topic being covered in the media and the posted material not ending up buried in the large pile that lands on the editor-in-chief's desk each day.
2. Relevant newspapers, magazines and broadcasts are monitored to see if the topic has been covered and, if so, whether the reporting is to the client's advantage. If the topic has been ignored or if the client has been represented negatively, the PR officer must examine their own approach carefully and decide how to redress the balance by achieving positive publicity. Print cuttings and broadcast recordings are sent to the client to show how well the PR officer is working.
3. Writing press releases and producing other promotional material, such as brochures and leaflets, appropriate to the client and audience. This is a form of journalistic writing in that the writing style is similar. The message has to come across quickly and clearly. However, as the aim of the material is to promote the interests of that organization alone, it will not feature anything that a journalist working for, say, a newspaper might use to balance the story, such as the views of protestors.

In an area that embodies about ten different jobs in one, it's fair to say that there is also no single set of ideal qualities or qualifications for entering this demanding field. Some skills get used more than others but, just like news, the unexpected can and invariably does happen and you need to be on the front line ready to deal with it. Here are some of the desirable attributes of a successful PR, as suggested by some leading employers.

*   Writing skills;
*   to prepare press releases, write articles, scripts;

- verbal skills;

- creative flair;

- broad vision;

- attention to detail;

- ability to study and analyse the businesses you are working for;

- ability to work well with people on all levels, media, management, colleagues;

- energy;

- numeracy.

One of the largest PR firms is that of the government, the Central Office of Information. It represents government departments in the same way that a private firm would represent a private company.

The Central Office of Information, or COI as it is more commonly known, is a Government agency with a network of eight regional offices covering the whole of England. The regional offices are North Eastern (Newcastle upon Tyne); Yorkshire and Humberside (Leeds); Eastern (Cambridge); London and South Eastern (London); North Western (Manchester); West Midlands (Birmingham); East Midlands (Nottingham); South Western (Bristol). Each regional office can deal with issues of national concern but with the added benefit of being able to give a local perspective. The regions also deal specifically with matters affecting their catchment area.

The COI provides press and publicity services mainly for government departments and other public-sector bodies. These 'clients' include the Royal Household; the Home Office, the Department of Transport; the Ministry of Defence; Training and Enterprise Councils (TECs); the Prime Minister's Office and the Vehicle Inspectorate.

Press offices working for the Government Information Service give a 24-hours-a-day, seven-days-a-week service and act as the link between the big government departments and the media. When a big story breaks, such as the announcement of new policies or a disaster on an oil rig, it is the job of the press officer to keep newspapers, radio and television stations both here and abroad informed. Even when nothing dramatic is taking place, a COI press officer would carry out the following tasks:

- write press releases;

- deal with media enquiries;

- organize media conferences;

- arrange interviews;

- accompany ministers on visits;

- maintain media contacts.

Recruits come from diverse backgrounds. Some may be media or communication studies graduates and others have prior media experience. Training is given on-the-job.

Public relations: training and entry routes

Public relations is such a large industry that many opportunities are opening up for entry at all levels. Some of the bigger agencies recruit graduates or even school-leavers and train them so it is worth contacting agencies directly for details. The content of in-house training varies from agency to agency but will include copywriting, handling accounts, media relations and business practice. The Institute of Public Relations has a detailed list of degrees, certificates and diplomas, seminars and short courses providing training in public relations at all levels. It can also tell you which PR consultancies have in-house graduate training programmes. Contact them at IPR, The Old Trading House, 15 Northburgh Street, London EC1V 0PR (0171 253 5151).

Many highly successful journalists spend their entire careers never working for a specific newspaper, magazine, radio or television station. As the future heralds an increasingly freelance culture and the need for diversification, many more will be investigating these and other pathways to a career in journalism.

9

The mechanics of getting a media job

If you are still convinced, after reading of the agonies and ecstasies of a career in journalism, that you want to break in, it's never too soon to take that first step up the ladder. Employers are looking for long-standing commitment and proven aptitude even from first-time applicants these days. From speaking to a variety of editors working in different media, it is clear that there are typical characteristics which they look for, ranging from good writing ability to a positive attitude. At the same time, they are looking for a spark of individuality that makes you stand out from other candidates who have identical skills to you.

It sounds a cliché but there is no one way in to journalism. But the adjectives which characterize most would-be reporters' job hunting are persistence, determination, patience, dedication and, most of all, luck. This book cannot help with the last factor on that list, but it can give you the experience of others and a few pointers to help you make that break. So whether you are hunting for your first job or hoping for a spell of work experience, read on.

BEFORE YOU EVEN CONSIDER APPLYING ...

As in just about every profession today, thousands are competing for fewer jobs in journalism, so it is essential that potential employees know how to shine. Many people are well-qualified to become journalists but, as any editor will tell you, it takes more than paper qualifications to land that sought-after job.

It takes determination, commitment, stamina, a spark of individuality and a good eye for a story to make an editor take a second glance.

In the process of writing this book, dozens of editors, managers and reporters were interviewed and asked for their advice on what makes a good journalist. The answer was clear. No matter how much technology progresses and no matter how fiercely competitive the industry becomes, there are still basic qualities which every journalist must have whatever medium they hope to work within.

In an industry which is intended to present information factually and objectively, there is no doubt subjectivity reigns on the part of editors and employers over what sort of person they would like to take on. Rightly or wrongly, certain characteristics arise again and again. Typically, these include having a degree, being aged under 25 and single for a first job with personality traits such as confidence and authority. But each editor was keen to stress there are exceptions to the rule in every newsroom and that it is basically down to how well the prospective journalist performs at interview. For instance, one regional evening newspaper employs a former footballer who suffered an injury and decided to move into news. In another example, a national television news producer with no formal journalistic training worked her way up from being a receptionist at a local radio station. It can be done and any editor will tell you that if you are determined enough and willing to learn, you can break your way in, but it takes time, plenty of knocks along the way and a great deal of patience and motivation when the going gets rough.

Of the editors interviewed, these are the main attributes that most of them cited:

1. You must be able to present information clearly and simply with spotless spelling, punctuation and grammar.
2. You must have an unparalleled interest in all aspects of humanity and have a fascination for people in all walks of life and their lives. You should be able to exhibit a genuine interest in current affairs.
3. You must be sensible and have sound judgment, which is often assessed at interview by asking you how you would respond in a specific situation, and be able to write balanced copy objectively.
4. You must be prepared to devote your life to the pursuit of news, work very unsociable hours and be prepared to subordinate your private life to journalism.

5. You have to be able to work fast and accurately with acute attention to detail.
6. You have to be a good communicator and listener but assertive enough to refuse to take 'no' for an answer.
7. You must be able to face moral dilemmas and be prepared to conform to editorial demands even if it is against your own wishes or principles.
8. Lastly, and perhaps most importantly, you should have a healthy disrespect for authority and question everything that is considered common sense.

A local paper's Night News Editor says he'd look for somebody who was bubbling with enthusiasm for life and displays vibrancy, energy, determination and a love of language:

> A journalist has got to be outside the herd to succeed. On a practical level, the hours make it difficult to mix with people and you shouldn't be part of a political or commercial group because influences will come to bear on you which will be embarrassing to break.

Because competition is so fierce, whichever route you choose, it helps to be able to illustrate your commitment with prior experience. Higher education institutions are full of student publications and closed-circuit radio and TV stations so you must get involved. Most successful journalists started out on their student rag. However bad it is, and many are excellent and win awards, involvement shows initiative and the willingness to do more with your three years than sit in seminars and go to the pub. Sadly, student apathy and a lack of funds means that some institutions do not have a thriving publication. If that is the case, start your own. Try to get funds from the students union. You will need an office and some basic equipment plus money to print or photocopy. Get a team together and go out and get sponsorship and advertising. Make sure it is well designed and written. Students working in a wide range of disciplines would benefit from working on the design, marketing and distribution as well as the editorial.

Cuttings

It is an irony, but unavoidable nonetheless, that you will almost always be expected to show evidence of journalistic experience in order to get your first job! You need to have a cuttings file that illustrates you have been determined to get into journalism long before applying for the post. A poem from the school magazine is not going to be enough; you need to have had something published or broadcast in a wider context. So how on earth do you get your first story in? Remember there are many people competing with you to get their copy in print so you have to handle the situation professionally. It helps if you do some background research into the newspaper itself before approaching newsdesks as this will show editors that you have the care and initiative to do the job properly. Don't be too ambitious by trying to get your story in *The Times,* unless it is a massive exclusive, of course. The local weekly paper will be more grateful and give you a better 'show' and perhaps a by-line. An article in the weekly paper should be sufficient to impress radio editors, as long as you can say how you would treat the story as a sound package. But even getting something in your local paper is hard as there are many competing with you for space.

Local newspapers are often on the lookout for local correspondents or stringers. These are people who contribute weekly information about what is happening within their particular community. This may range from school concerts to minor council issues and gives you the chance to get your work in print and gain experience and contacts. This kind of work helps you to develop your own news sense and learn how to liaise with a newsdesk which is a skill in its own right, especially if you ever need to sell a story to a national. An interest in sport is useful as many papers rely on stringers to submit copy on matches and other sporting pursuits. It's no use trying to cover the big football league match, as that will invariably be covered by staff with press passes and tickets to the executive bar. But Sunday league soccer, boxing and unfortunately most women's sporting events will not normally be covered in-house so your help may be welcomed. You may get paid a pittance but these cuttings, particularly if they bear your by-line, are priceless. Here's how to go about it:

1. First, have an idea. You may hear of something unusual in your community which you feel is newsworthy to the targeted readership. Make sure it has not been covered already by sifting through back issues in the library. Then try

to come up with an angle, that is, the most newsworthy aspect of the story which will catch the editor's – and the readers' – attention.

2. Once you have the idea, make sure it is workable by knowing that you will be able to gain access to the relevant spokespeople and research. It's no use suggesting an exclusive about a local vice ring if non-one will ever confirm it to you or comment on it. This is making sure you can 'stand the story up'.

3. Study your target outlet. How long do articles tend to be? Are they written in a particular style? Try to stick to this as much as possible.

4. Once convinced your story will stand up, telephone the editor and explain who you are and ask if they would be interested in your story. If you tend to be nervous on the telephone, write down a script beforehand to put beside the telephone to remind you of the points you want to discuss so you come across as confident and cheerful, rather than hesitant.

5. If they accept, ask in what format they would like the work presented and to what deadline. Bigger papers may ask you to file over the telephone to a copytaker. A weekly may be happy with copy typed on one side of A4 paper, double-line spaced with a catchword (a one-word title to identify your story instantly to the newsdesk, sub-editors, etc.), date of publication and your name. It may help the newsdesk if you also include names and telephone numbers of your contacts. However, if and when you start being paid for your contributions you can ask to be paid extra for contact details.

6. Don't ask to be paid, not the first time anyway. The column inches are more valuable to you than the chance of a fiver at this stage in your career.

Work placements

It's not what you know it's who you know. Yes, we hear this little phrase everywhere, especially from parents and teachers encouraging us to make contacts. In journalism, it really is a bit of both. Just because the editor of the local radio station is your uncle's brother-in-law's wife does not mean you can hassle her for a job. But, as very few journalism jobs are advertised, it pays to get yourself known. Letters of application pour into newsrooms every day and if you are lucky they get filed or are used to wedge up a rocky table. The people who get taken on are the ones who are persistent and whose name has become familiar and trustworthy to staff. As a start, see if you can get at least a chance to look round the newspaper/magazine/radio/TV office. While there, chat to staff and ask for their advice on how to go about getting a placement and where would be best to try. See the following section on applications for advice on making contact.

If you do get a work placement, remember that journalists can despise work experience people. They may be nice to you, give you some fillers to write and take you out on a job, but secretly they wish you weren't there. Well at least that's the case if you sit sullenly at your desk staring into mid-air, reluctantly make a cup of tea only when asked and never say a word. If however, you answer the telephone, offer to sort out the cuttings file, offer story ideas and generally behave like a friendly and intelligent person you will do fine. A lacklustre work experience candidate can be a millstone to the smooth operation of a newsroom and as they aren't in short supply of candidates because schools and colleges farm them out for a fortnight with stunning regularity, make sure that you make the most of it. There's always someone to replace you. A good work experience person always makes a positive impact and is remembered and may even get a reference. If the newsroom is busy and you are genuinely being ignored despite your enthusiasm and endless coffee-making, this is what you can do to while away the hours and impress your colleagues:

1. Offer to write fillers which are one or two paragraph stories important in their own right and also used to fill gaps between stories on newspaper pages. These are time-consuming when you have main leads to do so get the reporters to sort through their in-trays. They may have some pictures that need captioning as well.
2. Offer to do a vox pop. This is where you go into the street and ask a random selection of members of the public their views of a particular issue, from pollution to football. These are time-consuming to journalists but add flavour to a newspaper or radio bulletin and would be well-received. They also give you the chance to illustrate and practise your interviewing and writing skills.

3. Ask if you can shadow a member of staff such as a sub-editor. They may take you to where the paper is printed and show you the production process in action or teach you a little of the rudiments of subbing which looks great on your CV. Or go out with a photographer and see what they get up to. As a journalist, there is more and more call for you to be multi-skilled. You certainly need to be able to communicate with people in other departments than your own.
4. Ask if any advertising features need writing. On a weekly paper, advertisements will sometimes be accompanied by editorial. Reporters often don't like doing these because they feel producing material of a commercial nature compromises their journalistic objectivity so your help would be welcomed.

Afterwards, keep in touch on a regular basis, letting them know what you are doing and seeing if you can assist with any particular project.

The News Producer at Sky News advises that work placement candidates don't make a pest of themselves because everyone is so busy. Don't be pushy, she warns, because the commonly held belief that foot-in-the-door types land journalism jobs is not true. You are more likely to be invited back if you are polite, calm and competent.

Other useful skills

There are other valuable skills which you can easily gain which can make all the difference to your application. Wordprocessing, typing and shorthand are things you are either taught or pick up on the job, but prior knowledge would show some initiative. Most journalists type in a very haphazard way but to a high speed. It's obviously better for your accuracy and the health of your hands if you can learn to do it properly. Confidence with wordprocessors is an advantage. Systems used by news organizations vary but being faced with a VDU screen for the first time can be rather daunting and can frighten some people away from entering the industry. A few local evening classes in wordprocessing can build up your confidence and typing speed and look good on your CV.

Shorthand training can be the bane of a journalist's life. Local newspaper trainees often have to travel to weekly classes in the evenings for hours of drilling. You should attain a speed of 100wpm but, like driving, some people pick it up quickly whereas for others it is an uphill struggle. It may help to find a night class beforehand to build up some speed even if you do not take an exam. Although many journalists use tape recorders, they tend to use them only as back-up as machines can break down, especially when exposed to rainstorms. And, as stated earlier, most editors are impressed by candidates who have taken the traditional approach and who have grounded themselves in this basic skill.

It cannot be stressed strongly enough how most candidates fare better when they can prove their dedication to the field of journalism through work experience and samples of their own writing. However, there are many who can disprove this point so do not be deterred from applying for jobs as employers who see potential in a recruit will be prepared to give them a chance. So where are media posts advertised?

Where to look

Well, in fact, most media jobs are unadvertised and vacancies are filled by individuals who have applied speculatively or have made themselves known to the organization through work experience or freelancing. If you are planning on applying for a job on spec, these are some of the places you might look for names of employers but be sure to telephone to check names and addresses are not out of date:

Benn's Media Directory (annual)
Willings Press Guide (annual)
Writers' and Artists' Yearbook (annual)

These can be found in the reference section of most libraries.

If you have a geographical area in mind, London for example, check telephone directories for publishers and broadcasters.

Media jobs are advertised in the following publications but may also crop up elsewhere so do not treat this list as exhaustive. Many will be available in libraries or they can be obtained from newsagents. It is worth asking school or college librarians whether they will subscribe to any of these publications as they can be expensive.

Broadcast
Campaign
UK Press Gazette
Magazine Week
Media Week
TV Week
Journalist's Week
The Guardian
The Independent
The Journalist
Sight and Sound
Stage and Television Today
TV Buyer
Audio Visual

BBC jobs and training opportunities are advertised in the national media and a summary usually appears on CEEFAX.

YOUR APPLICATION

Remember that a journalist is a writer and presenter of information and therefore your application should be impeccable in both content and appearance. How you sell yourself and your interest in journalism is crucial, whether you are applying for a high-powered job, a training course or a work placement. If you are to be invited for interview, you must make a good first impression on paper. Speculative applications can be fruitful and most media posts are awarded this way. But do not send off forms and letters like confetti – your applications should be direct and well-aimed towards specific organizations if they are to be well-received. If you answer a job advertisement, particularly for a major organization, you may be asked to fill out an application form. Where possible, you should type this as it shows you have made some effort toward presentation. Any supplementary sheets, for example where candidates are asked to write a review or other piece, should also be typed or wordprocessed and carefully attached to the main form. It looks well-organized and is a sign of a well-organized mind. Your covering letter, however, may sometimes be handwritten, particularly if you have neat writing, and definitely if asked for in the advertisement, as it shows a personal touch. State the title of the job you are applying for and where you saw the advertisement. If you do not have an application form to fill out, and you are contacting an organization on a speculative basis, your approach should consist of two, maybe three sections:

1. your covering letter;
2. your curriculum vitae;
3. any cuttings or samples of work.

Covering letter

Your letter should be short, to the point and accurate. It should be written on good, white A4-size paper with your address, telephone number and date on the top right hand side of the sheet and that of the addressee lower down on the left. Try not to start off with 'Dear Sir/Madam'. You should aim to identify a key individual within the organization and address them personally. The editor or news editor is the best bet and it will only take one short telephone call to their switchboard to check their name and its spelling. Your letter should be on one side of A4 only and should spell out clearly what you are asking for. Remember, you want to be a journalist so be direct and unambiguous but don't be too pushy.

Something along the lines of this for an opening paragraph might help:

> I am writing to ask you to consider me for the post of ...... should a vacancy arise within your organization. Please find enclosed my curriculum vitae which details my experience to date.

You should be clear about the kind of work you are looking for. Don't just say you want to work in newspapers, specify whether you are interested in news reporting, feature writing or whatever. Your next paragraph could explain why you are keen to work for that specific publication/station/programme and state briefly what skills you could bring to it. Send in your application quickly with every 'i' dotted and 't' crossed. You may want to finish off on a pro-active note:

> If there aren't any vacancies currently, could I come in for a chat to discuss possibilities or undertake work experience or temporary work?

That should at least help to get you in and get your face known.

Personal preference of the editor dictates whether they like to see covering letters handwritten or typed. Handwritten letters, if neat and well-organized, show you have made a personal effort, not just changed the name and company at the top of a file on your wordprocessor. But there is now a swing towards typed letters, especially if your handwriting is illegible, no matter how neatly laid out your letter may be.

Curriculum vitae

This is a summary of your personal details, education and experience to date. Usually produced on one or two sides of A4, it should be arranged so that it looks neat and professional and so that the reader can clearly pick out the information they need. It should be impeccably typed or preferably word-processed because that exhibits flair with new technology, especially if you highlight headings and important points. If using a computer, don't fall prey to the typefaces in the menu – stick to something plain and simple. (Times Roman 11pt is wonderful for a CV as is Helvetica. Avoid using typefaces that are too fancy.)

Information should come under a few simple headings but you can experiment with layouts to find the best for you. The main headings tend to be:

Personal details: including full name, address, telephone number, date of birth, driver's licence, nationality;

Education: schools/colleges attended and dates, qualifications/grades gained;

Employment history or work experience: dates, name and address of employer, job title and main duties.

The information is usually listed in reverse order with the most recent details first. So if you've got a postgraduate qualification, list that before your degree, then your schooling. If you have done relevant work experience at an organization be sure to make the best of it on your CV.

Other relevant information: This is where you can mention any skills you have.

Interests: This section should show a good mix of personal and social pursuits – listening to records alone is not enough for most jobs!

Referees: Names and addresses of at least two – one personal and one work/education related.

Try to include any **supplementary material** to prove your abilities. Ideally, you will have a few cuttings which have been published. Photocopies of these should be displayed imaginatively, not folded up in an envelope or in a child's scrapbook. That would suggest you did not have much pride in what you had done. There's no standard way of displaying cuttings but slipped inside a clear plastic A4 wallet inside a ringbinder or album will keep them neat and flat.

If you do not have any examples of published work, improvise. For instance, one graduate applying for his first job as a current affairs director did not have a showreel so he submitted his file of college photography to show he had a good eye and could represent an issue or event pictorially. He got the job. Showing imagination and individuality can get you noticed while other applications blend into the background.

A newspaper editor's advice for applicants

You need to show some flair and attention to detail. It's amazing the number of CVs and letters which come in which are illegible, scruffy or contain spelling mistakes. These would seem to suggest the applicant isn't really terribly bothered. The second thing to bear in mind is that if in some way you can make your application stand out from the crowd you are giving yourself a head start. When we begin our search for graduate trainees we literally receive hundreds of letters and forms. The person who gets noticed is the person who finds some new twist on the whole procedure to say, 'Hey, look, I'm an interesting person.' Something eye-catching that makes you feel this application isn't like the last half-dozen that you went through. Sometimes that can be gimmicky but part of the trick of getting noticed in the media world is to come up with a new idea or to successfully recycle an old idea.

Follow-up calls

Once you have sent off your application, it is a good idea a few days later to 'phone and check it was received safely. Do not make a pest of yourself but ask politely whether they have had a chance to consider your application and whether you could come in for a chat. It shows initiative and determination.

Interviews for journalism jobs

It is virtually unheard of for anyone to get a media job without having an interview. While you might look the perfect candidate on paper, the company wants to be sure that they can work with you as an individual and that you can operate well in a stressful situation.

The format for interviews varies. Some will be very relaxed and informal. You will sit around a table with usually three or four company representatives, say the managing editor, editor, someone from personnel and perhaps a reporter. They will try to put you at ease because they want to reach the real you, not a nervous wreck! Other interviews, particularly for very large organizations, may take place in two stages, the second only if you are shortlisted. These are more formal and you may have to face a panel of interviewers.

Try to look the part and wear what journalists working for that organization might wear. Wearing a business suit is not recommended in every case as it can look too formal and detract from what you are saying. However, if you are applying to be a business journalist, it would be essential. Try to look smart and authoritative. Wear the kind of outfit that would enable you to feel comfortable in any situation with any person you might meet on a report. Don't wear jeans!

Don't go empty-handed. You have your original cuttings and by this time might have further examples of work to show.

Have a think beforehand about how you will respond to questions. The panel will want to see someone who is quick and confident with a controlled sense of humour, not over-pushy and not too nervous. Always have an answer; don't say 'I don't know' and try not to answer with one-word replies.

It is quite normal at interviews to be asked to discuss a current affairs issue. It is a common complaint that many candidates tend to read all the papers from a few days before the interview. This knowledge is superficial. What editors really want to see is genuine long-term commitment to current affairs so that it is clear you understand situations locally, at home and abroad in some depth. You may be asked to come up with story ideas there and then. Prepare beforehand and if you do not get asked, mention them at an appropriate time. Also suggest who you would use as spokespeople and how you might angle the story. Radio and television journalist job interviews will often require the candidate to produce a treatment for a story on paper, including a short cue or script and a breakdown of how the package would be structured.

Typical interview questions include:

1. Why do you want to work here?
2. What specific skills can you offer?
3. What are your ambitions?
4. A trick question often asked is: what would you like to be if you weren't a journalist? If you can think of another career you'll be crossed off the list.
5. Hypothetical questions sometimes arise, for example, someone has just telephoned the newsdesk to say they've seek a UFO land. Your deadline is in half an hour. What would you do next? An appropriate answer might be that you would question the caller to discover whether they seem reputable. Are they alone or are there other witnesses you could speak to? If the caller seems genuine you would consult the news editor who would probably advise you to contact the emergency services to find out whether they are aware of the reports. If so, what information do they have at this stage? Telephone shops, businesses or other contacts near the alleged scene of the event of see if they noticed any activity. Contact airports, and so on. If you are ever in any doubt about how you would approach a story, do not reply, 'I don't know'. Say that you would seek the advice of the newsdesk or editor as that shows you are sensible and would not tackle something if you felt out of your depth.

Don't always feel you have to agree with the interviewer. They often ask leading questions to see how you react. So if they openly question the way you would cover a story, but you are sure your idea would work, stick to your guns and explain your viewpoint. Most of all stay calm, think clearly and be polite – that is what the editor will expect when they send you out to represent their organization.

Editors are looking for the person with the sort of personality that will help a young journalist go out and meet all sorts of different people in a variety of situations and will work well in an informal but friendly team environment. Journalism is a very competitive type of work which isn't going to attract people who want a regimented nine-to-five existence. It's always going to need people who can think or breathe news 24 hours a day. It's a job you never leave behind. All our mistakes and failures appear in public so a journalist must have scrupulous attention to detail and be prepared to dedicate time and patience to ensure they get their stories right.

Always try to have a couple of questions to ask at the end of the interview which should not relate to how much time you get off. Make them something pro-active, like asking about promotion opportunities or in-house training. You can also enquire what the next stage of the selection process is and when you are likely to hear the outcome.

Follow-up letter

It is always a good idea to send a short letter the day after your interview (any longer and they'll have made their decision) thanking them for the meeting and re-affirming your commitment to the position and the company. That way, you'll stay in their minds.

Whatever the outcome of the interview, it has been a most valuable experience. In fact, to be shortlisted for interview at all is an achievement in itself. So do not be too deflated if you have not been successful this time. Don't dwell on the experience but learn from it and you will be better prepared next time.

The pace of change is so rapid that any would-be journalist should acquire as broad a range of skills as possible and assume that it's all change from that point on. Some will go into a particular title or branch of the media and stay there but many more will switch around and will find their working week will consist of three or four different jobs.

Technological advancement has made viable an enormous range of publications and broadcasting services. One of the plus-points of working in the media is that it is one area of the economy that is exploding. Every medium appears to be under threat – in fact it would seem that traditional ideas about television being the 'superior' journalistic format are seriously drawn into question by the rise of the computer as the new medium. But for the journalist, the information provider, you are a winner either way because the more outlets that exist the more means of delivery there is for your work. While the people manufacturing newsprint might see the electronic media as a threat, all young journalists see it as an opportunity because you are lucky to be in a business where opportunities do seem to be widening all the time.

Good luck!

Further reading

PRINT JOURNALISM

Aitchison, J. (1989) *Writing for the Press*, Stanley Thornes, Cheltenham.

Hodgson, F.W. (1984) *Modern Newspaper Practice*, Butterworth-Heinemann, Oxford.

BROADCAST JOURNALISM

Boyd, A. (1993) *Broadcast Journalism*, Focal Press, Oxford.

Yorke, I. (1990) *Basic TV Reporting*, Focal Press, Oxford.

Yorke, I. (1995) *Television News*, Focal Press, Oxford.

GENERAL INFORMATION

Peak, S. (1992) *The Media Guide*, Fourth Estate, London.

Index